Nothing but God

Nothing but God

The Everyday Mysticism of Meister Eckhart

L. J. MILONE

RESOURCE *Publications* · Eugene, Oregon

NOTHING BUT GOD
The Everyday Mysticism of Meister Eckhart

Resource Publications
An Imprint of Wipf and Stock Publishers
199 W. 8th Ave., Suite 3
Eugene, OR 97401

www.wipfandstock.com

PAPERBACK ISBN: 978-1-5326-7173-9
HARDCOVER ISBN: 978-1-5326-7174-6
EBOOK ISBN: 978-1-5326-7175-3

Manufactured in the U.S.A.   MARCH 7, 2019

This book is dedicated to my family:
Jessica, Amelia, Therese, Rachel, and Joseph. I love you!

Contents

Acknowledgments

THERE ARE MANY PEOPLE to thank for their support in writing, editing, and completing this book on Meister Eckhart. First, I want to thank the community of the Maryland and Washington, DC chapter of Contemplative Outreach. They gave me two opportunities to offer a series of retreats on Meister Eckhart. The wonderful people who attended were incredibly supportive through their silent prayer and deep engagement with the spirituality of Meister Eckhart. Second, I want to thank a major influence over this book, friend and editor Steve Thompson. He generously dedicated many hours to talking through the content and advising me on changes to the book both large and small. His help was invaluable. Most of all, I want to thank my family and friends for the support, my parents in particular. Above all, I am utterly grateful for my my loving wife, Jessica, and my beautiful children, Amelia, Therese, and our twins: Rachel and Joseph. The presence of God is palpable in the love of family.

Introduction

As often as we can, my family enjoys taking walks. We amble along the well-maintained paths in our neighborhood whatever the season. Over our many walks, we've gotten caught in the rain and blocked by the snow. We've meandered and changed course. Our four-year-old daughter, Amelia, has run off the path to pick a flower, look at a bug, or examine some piece of trash. Jessica, my wife, enjoys the fresh air as well as the exercise. Therese, our two-year-old, falls fast asleep in fresh air. It's good, simple, and free family time. The path we take is clearly defined, well laid out, and has no obstacles. All we have to do is leave our house and go.

Spiritual living is also about walking along a path. In its earliest days Christianity was called "the way," for Jesus called people to follow him along a path into God. Jesus teaches a way of spiritual living, a path. All we have to do is take the path. We may meander, get lost, or get caught in difficult life situations, but as long as we stay on the path we will know, as Jesus promises, the love of God.

Throughout the history of Christianity, many different people have defined further the path of Jesus. Some, like Francis of Assisi, have brought Christianity into clearer focus. Others have obscured it, locking it up in cathedrals, convents, or monasteries. There are other guides, though, who have helped us reconnect with the path of Jesus in radically powerful ways. One of these guides is Meister Eckhart.

WHO IS MEISTER ECKHART?

Meister Eckhart was a Catholic mystic and Dominican friar who lived in medieval Germany. A mystic is someone who relates to God directly and is transformed by the experience. Meister Eckhart enjoyed a direct relationship with God and it totally changed him. The joy, freedom, and identity he received from God propelled him into a life of sharing the Good News of divine joy with the people of his time. As a Dominican friar, he shared the Good News by preaching. In his preaching, he proclaimed deep mystical truths to everyday people.

Around 1260 Meister Eckhart was born to a family of the lower aristocracy in the Germanic region of Thuringia. He likely entered the Dominican order in the late 1270's. After higher studies at the University of Paris, the Dominican leadership sent Eckhart to Erfurt, Germany, in the fall of 1294 to be the prior of the Dominican community there. Then, in 1302 Eckhart returned to Paris to take up the external Dominican chair of theology at the University of Paris, thus earning the title "Master" of theology, which is "Meister" in medieval German. The new Meister then came back to Germany to serve as the first provincial of a newly created province, Saxonia from 1303 to 1311. The next few decades, Eckhart bounced between the University of Paris and administrative duties in the Dominican Order. Notably he spent time in Strasbourg where, in addition to administration, he immersed himself in pastoral work: preaching, spiritual guidance, and offering care to the many women's communities in the city.

Then, in late 1323 Eckhart went to Cologne, the intellectual center of the German Dominicans. Many of his surviving German sermons come from his stay in Cologne, from 1323 to 1327, during which time he traveled to Avignon to defend himself against accusations that his message was heretical. The accusations came from the archbishop of Cologne, Henry II of Virneburg. On September 26, 1326 Eckhart appeared before Henry's diocesan inquisition to defend himself against the charge of heresy.

Afterwards, Eckhart appealed his case to the pope, for only the pope— or the University of Paris in his place—could try a Master of theology like Eckhart. Since the pope at that time resided in Avignon, France, Meister Eckhart had to travel there to defend himself. Eckhart was able to undercut charges of heresy by being willing to renounce any errors ecclesiastical authorities discovered. This saved the Meister from being labeled a heretic. We will return to Eckhart's trial at a later point. It is important to note here that Eckhart, unlike the pope and his inquisitorial commission, had no qualms about presenting his mystical message to such an audience. He believed that the joy of divine oneness was the destiny of all, regardless of their status, education, or role in life.

Eckhart was a master of the spiritual life, and in more ways than one. In addition to being a preacher, he was an academic. In his day, one could be a "master of living" or a "master of learning." Eckhart was both an academic master and a spiritual master. He was a true theologian, speaking about God because he knew God.

Eckhart the spiritual master gives us a mystical path that brings us back to the core of the Gospel, which is knowing and loving God in Christ. Eckhart is serious about Jesus' saying: "this is eternal life, that they may know you, the only true God, and Jesus Christ whom you have sent" (John 17:3). As such, the path of Meister Eckhart is simple. He says to "delight in nothing but God."[1] The path of Meister Eckhart is the path of nothing but God: knowing, seeking, and loving God alone. According to Eckhart, God cannot wait for us to do so! He preaches:

> Never has a person longed after anything so intensely as God longs to bring a person to the point of knowing him. God is always ready but we are very unready. God is near to us but we are very far from him. God is within us but we are outside. God is at home in us but we are abroad . . . God help us that we all follow him so that he can bring us to the point where we truly know him.[2]

To know God, Eckhart says, we have to center on nothing but God. This means we have to follow Jesus in self-denial: "If any want to become my followers, let them deny themselves and take up their cross and follow me" (Mark 8:34). As Eckhart sees it, we focus on God by letting go of self. Eckhart preaches, "Now God wants no more from you than that you should in creaturely fashion go out of yourself, and let God be God in you."[3] The Meister extends a radical spiritual invitation to let ourselves go into the mystery of God.

Jesus figures into the path of Meister Eckhart centrally because Jesus is God in the flesh, God as a human being. Often, conventional Christianity stops at simply assenting to this mystery as a doctrine. Christians seems to hold this belief like an opinion, and that is enough. Such is not the case for Eckhart. For him, Jesus reveals our inherent oneness with God. This is essential to the Gospel and to Eckhart's path. We are always already one with God. This oneness, though, is repressed by a lot of mental, emotional, and spiritual junk. In a word, attachments are the problem. Eckhart, though,

1. Eckhart, *Meister Eckhart: The Essential Sermons*, 252.

2. Fox, *Passion for Creation*, 141.

3. Eckhart, *Meister Eckhart: The Essential Sermons*, 184.

reduces the problem to the self. *Who we think we are* gets in the way of *who we really are.* For Eckhart, we realize we are one with God by centering our hearts on nothing but God and by letting go of self or *who we think we are.* Eckhart preaches, "the soul wanting to perceive God must forget itself and lose itself."[4] This is his mystical path. This is also the subject of the present book, namely, centering on nothing but God here and now.

TOO PREOCCUPIED WITH STAR WARS!

How often are we not here and now? A few years ago, I was looking forward to the release of the brand new *Star Wars* movie, *The Force Awakens*, with great excitement. I was practically frothing at the mouth over this movie. I read articles online speculating about the plot of the movie and watched YouTube videos dedicated to *Star Wars* movie news. I almost got consumed with my anticipation for the new *Star Wars* movie. Then, the big day came. I saw *Star Wars: The Force Awakens* on Christmas day in 2015. As I watched the movie, though, I grew increasingly dissatisfied. I did not like the plot. I did not like the new characters. I felt afraid to admit that it might be the first *Star Wars* movie I did not like. Afterwards, I was haunted by how I felt about it. Again and again, I reviewed scenes from the movie. Eagerly, I sought out critical reviews of the movie, along with fan reactions. Nothing helped. Eventually I had to admit I did not like the movie.

Both my avid anticipation and begrudging dislike of the new *Star Wars* movie kept me from acknowledging what was going on right in front of me. I ignored the present moment. I think many of us do this. We get preoccupied with future and past and so fail to live in the here and now. My focus on future and past in the form of *Star Wars* often kept me from enjoying my life as it unfolded in the present moment. There were times when I was not present to my family, friends, or work because I was too busy fuming internally about *Star Wars.*

I wonder how many of us act like I did? How often do we get trapped in future and past experiences? How often do we miss out on the delights of the now? This is the only life you and I will ever live, yet we are constantly escaping the now by living too much in our heads through memory, fantasy, or anxiety. Life has a tendency, though, to happen when we are not looking. It passes us by while we stand in the corner ruminating over past

---

4. Fox, *Passion for Creation*, 140.

mistakes or fretting about future responsibilities. We miss God who is one with us right here and right now.

A FAITHFUL DISCIPLE OF JESUS

The Gospel of Mark rushes to the cross. In its sixteen short chapters, no one truly understands who Jesus is, and therefore who they really are, until the cross. Matthew's Gospel focuses on Jesus the teacher. His teachings all reflect entering the kingdom of heaven, loving like God, and letting go of whatever is in the way. Luke proclaims Jesus' universal gift of salvation while showing how prayerful, detached, and joyful life in Christ is. The Gospel of John reveals Jesus' identity as *I Am*, one with God the Father. Then, John reports, Jesus prays we might be just as one with God, too (John 17:20–21). All of these Gospel themes are central to the message of Meister Eckhart.

Although we have numerous sermons, treatises, and scripture commentaries from Meister Eckhart, his thinking revolves around a few recurring themes. Meister Eckhart's message is simple: "If you truly have God and only God, nothing will disturb you."[5] This is what he wants to communicate to us. If we have nothing but God in our hearts and minds, we will know peace. To have nothing but God is to be detached and one with God. We are one with God, but we do not know it. To know it, we have to detach. To know *nothing but God* is to know infinite joy. This is the teaching of Jesus. The Meister is presenting the Gospel in a way that attracted a wide medieval audience. His way of preaching the Gospel message has, I believe, the potential to attract a wide contemporary audience as well.

Centering on nothing but God is the whole practical point of Meister Eckhart's mystical path. How do we focus on God alone? How do we let go to realize oneness with God in Christ? What is it like to be one with God? Who is this God, anyway? Also, how can I walk this mystical path in my hectic, stressful, and everyday life? With Meister Eckhart's help, we will reflect on these questions throughout the book. Meister Eckhart uses five themes to unpack his mystical path: the ground, detachment, the breakthrough, the birth of the Word in our souls, and living without a why. Underneath these themes and at the core of his preaching, Eckhart is committed to letting God be God. This means he respects God's incomprehensible mystery. God transcends words, thinking, and even existence itself.

5. Chilson, *God Awaits You*, 42.

Still, Meister Eckhart's mystical path is within everyone's reach despite how anyone's life might look.

A MYSTICAL PATH

Meister Eckhart appears from across the centuries to help us enjoy this very moment fully and enjoy it now. He guides us into a new awareness, one that sees God in the ins and outs of our family time, professional lives, and every other part of our day. Meister Eckhart says the joy of the Lord is available to us right now. While preaching, Meister Eckhart once quipped:

> Do not be afraid, for this joy is close to you and is in you: there is not one of you who is so coarse-grained, so feeble of understanding, or so remote but he may find this joy within himself, in truth, as it is, with joy and understanding, before you leave this church today, indeed before I have finished preaching: he can find this as truly within him, live and possess it.[6]

We can know the joy of God within us and we can know it here and now.

In this book I describe Meister Eckhart's mystical path as "nothing but God." Even though he is easily misunderstood, Meister Eckhart's path is very simple: intend, seek, delight in, love, and know nothing but God. Often, Meister Eckhart refers to his path as practicing detachment. Detachment is the counterpart to seeking nothing but God. With our eyes set on nothing but God, we simultaneously stop paying attention to the things that get in the way. These things, for Eckhart, are not physical things but mental things: our attitudes, our compulsions, and our over-identification with thoughts and feelings. Our thinking gets in the way of the joy of the Lord. It was not the *Star Wars* movie itself that prevented me from enjoying the now, but my thinking about it. Over and over, Eckhart calls us back to the divine presence in the now, which means we let go of our thinking to pay attention to God now.

AN ACCESSIBLE SPIRITUALITY

Perhaps at this point, you're thinking, "Sounds great, but I have kids to raise, bills to pay, and responsibilities to keep"? So many of us are just trying to make it through the day. We are treading water, almost drowning in an

---

6. Eckhart, *Meister Eckhart: The Essential Sermons*, 61.

overwhelming ocean of expectations, obligations, guilt and shame feelings, and unfulfilled desires. We do our best to catch up on all the things we have to do. There does not seem to be enough time in a single day. Busy-ness is the name of our game. Spirituality can seem impossible in such a life. Meister Eckhart, however, testifies to the very real possibility of spiritual existence amidst busy-ness. As a preacher, teacher, counsellor, and administrator, Eckhart had many responsibilities. He likely felt the stress of being busy. Still, he points us to the center, to God our happiness, in the middle of our hectic lives. Eckhart says we can be one with God while active in the world. He gives us a spirituality of daily life.

No matter what we experience, Eckhart is convinced God is with us, within us, and one with us. God is utterly present and available in all things. All that is needed is to seek God alone. The Meister preaches, "I once thought . . . that a man should be so wholly detached in his intention that he had nobody and nothing in view but the Godhead in itself—neither salvation nor this or that, but just God as God."[7] Eckhart is a God-centered mystic. This God, though, is not the divinity of traditional religion, which is bound by beliefs, ideas, images, and rituals. Eckhart brings out the God of radical mystery, the God beyond religion. It is imperative for Eckhart that we focus on this God, the only God that exists!

The Meister is a clear example of an apophatic mystic, that is, a mystic who seriously focuses on the reality that no word, name, image, feeling, or thought can grasp God. As transcendent and infinite mystery, God is beyond all things. Therefore, all our language and thinking about God must be left behind to know God in truth. The apophatic tradition is the wayless way to God, transcending thoughts, words, and images to open to God in darkness, silence, and unknowing because God is supremely mysterious. It is a path with roots in Scripture's prohibition of worshiping any false images and Jesus' uprooting of the many idols good religious people worship instead of God as God really is.

Meister Eckhart is part of a living apophatic tradition. Dionysius the Areopagite and John Scottus Eriugena came before him. *The Cloud of Unknowing* and St. John of the Cross come after Eckhart. This tradition continues today through the writings of Thomas Merton and the practices of Centering Prayer, Christian Meditation, the Jesus prayer, and *Lectio Divina*.

These mystics of the apophatic tradition refer to the path to God as a way of nothingness. Most of them even refer to God as nothingness. God

---

7. Eckhart, *The Complete Mystical Works of Meister Eckhart*, 264.

is literally no-thing. More radically, since the divine nature is infinitely transcendent, God is nothingness beyond all being. Eckhart deepens this Christian tradition of divine nothingness. He is not denying the existence of God, but shocking our religious sensibilities so we realize just how different and transcendent God truly is. The divine is so mysterious and transcendently different from all existence that we can refer to God as the divine nothing.

Since no thought or experience can ever comprehend the incomprehensible, the Meister recommends silence, stillness, and detachment from mental forms to know the mystery of God. This emphasis on interior silence, mystery, unknowing, and letting go connect the medieval Meister to contemporary Christian contemplative practices, especially the practice called Centering Prayer. This is a way of prayer that enables us to commune with God beyond all thinking and in the silence of faith. From the beginning, the Christian tradition has taught contemplation, which is the sheer gift of God's very self to us as well as our total opening to and receiving of this infinite gift. Centering Prayer is this tradition updated for our time, which aims to open practitioners to the mystery by letting go of thinking and resting in God. One of the main teachers of Centering Prayer is the Trappist monk Thomas Keating. He writes, "The method of centering prayer is designed to turn off the ordinary flow of thoughts, that reinforces our habitual way of thinking of ourselves and of looking at the world."[8] Once we stop thinking, God's grace helps us to wake up to our inherent oneness with the divine. The point, though, is not to sit in meditation all day: "Not contemplative *prayer* but the contemplative *state* is the purpose of our practice . . . the permanent and abiding awareness of God."[9] Living in God all through the day—the contemplative state—is the essence of the Meister's message.

THIS LITTLE BOOK

Even though the Meister's whole life was determined by religion, his mystical path is open to religious and secular alike. Eckhart might be particularly engaging to anyone who has found traditional belief disconnected, bland, uninspiring, or unjust. To at least those disaffected from religion, the way we currently talk about and even worship God can come across as insipid

8. Keating, *Open Mind, Open Heart,* 120.
9. Keating, *Open Mind, Open Heart,* 102.

or unrelated to life. Eckhart may have had similar feelings. Many of the most popular pious trends in medieval Christendom—an extreme focus on the bleeding and tortured Christ, God as wrathful judge, or the expectation that preaching was supposed to convict a congregation of their sinfulness so they were roused to penance—are absent from the Meister's sermons. He bucked these and other widespread religious preoccupations by focusing on a deeper, more positive message. It is a message about God, Jesus, and the human person that both the secular and religious can enjoy. The Meister has much to offer anyone who is dissatisfied with religion and wants to be transformed, to anyone who desires to live in the Presence of the holy mystery yet gets turned off by the way our churches traditionally talk about God and Jesus.

Therefore, this will be a different book about Eckhart. Whereas most books mean to introduce the Meister and tend toward being scholarly overviews of his mystical themes, this book will reflect on Eckhart's path and how we might walk it as well. There will be a question haunting us: how do we live what Meister Eckhart preaches? While I will follow the general lines of contemporary Eckhart scholarship, I will depart from it at times with my own interpretation, which I hope brings out the relevance and practicality of Eckhart's path. To look at how we might walk the mystical path of Meister Eckhart also requires some digressions into how we live today, which concerns how we think, how we act, and what our collective issues are. This book will do this so we can see what it means to walk this mystical path in order to know God and to be transformed.

This book will explore Meister Eckhart's mystical path as a way of realizing the mystery of God—the divine nothingness—within the mundane of contemporary life. We will go about this exploration by way of five of his themes and his reverence for the mystery of God. Chapter 1, "God and Us," explores identity and Eckhart's explosive metaphor of the ground. Chapter 2, "Letting Go into God," focuses on the practice of letting go by way of Eckhart's themes of detachment and the breakthrough. Chapter 3, "God Becomes Real," takes up the issue of what living our oneness with God means and what it feels like through the birth and living without a why. Chapter 4, "Nothingness," looks at Eckhart's reverence for God's mystery and how the whole of his mysticism might be summarized with the word "nothing." Chapter 5 discusses the merchant mentality, a central concern of the Meister in one of his sermons and a major concern today. In chapter 6, we look at Eckhart's approach to the universal issue of suffering. Everything then feeds into chapter 7, "The Practice of Nothing but God," which examines how we might practice centering on nothing but God in daily life. Eckhart's path focuses on nothing else. It is both fiercely dedicated and light, simple, and full of joy. The conclusion, summarizing the most important points, then launches us back into daily life to walk the path of everyday mysticism, as my family walks around our neighborhood, namely with a quiet peace. Still, this path is a challenge because Eckhart is giving us the pure Gospel teaching on self-denial and losing one's life in the mold of Jesus (Mark 8:34–35).

The good Meister does not intend for us to be more religious in the sense of doing more church-related things. He invites us, rather, to contemplative living, which means realizing the mystery of God as we spend time with loved ones, drive to work, watch movies, play with our kids, vote, wait in line at the grocery store, and any of the million other things we do every single day. My hope and prayer is that this little book will help us to practice Meister Eckhart's mysticism, to walk his mystical path and so follow Jesus into oneness with God.

I

God and Us

MEISTER ECKHART'S MESSAGE IS simple. He tells us to center on nothing but God. This is what he wants to communicate to us. There is nothing but God and, so, seek and delight in nothing but God. If we have nothing but God in our hearts and minds, we will know peace. To have nothing but God is to be detached. It is to be one with God.

Meister Eckhart says we are always already one with God. But we don't know it or enjoy it. There are obstacles to our living oneness with God. This inherent unity with the divine is not real for us because we are so focused on ourselves. Once we let go of self, our oneness with God will become incredibly real for us. We realize our oneness with God by letting go. Three comments need to be made. First, God initiates, sustains, and completes this process of letting go. Second, God also brings about the realization of oneness. Divine grace starts, sustains, and ends the journey. Third, this oneness with God is what it means to be Christ. The oneness of humanity and divinity is the very essence of being Christ. When we realize oneness with God, by God's grace, we are Christ.

Here, then, lies the essence of Meister Eckhart's mysticism: we are one with God, but we do not know it. Our oneness with God becomes real for us by following Jesus in the practice of letting go, by keeping in mind nothing but God. Then, by the Holy Spirit, we discover our joyful oneness with God in Christ. Through our living this divine oneness, this Christ identity, God transforms the world.

Meister Eckhart uses a rich and explosive metaphor to communicate our incomprehensible oneness with God: the ground. The problem for Eckhart is we don't know we are always already one with God. We are disconnected from the ground, and, hence, from our true identity. The whole point of Meister Eckhart's path is to return to the ground. The ground answers the question "who am I?" For, in the ground we discover our identity in nothing but God.

THE PROBLEM OF GOD

Eckhart is a God-centered mystic, but there are good, honest, virtuous people who think God is a problem. These are our family members, our friends, and our co-workers. Our culture does not support belief in God, and sometimes neither do our churches! Still, Eckhart presents us with a spirituality wholly focused on God. This God, though, is not the God of conventional religion: a bland doctrinal divinity as conceived by banal and rigid religion. Eckhart brings out the God of radical mystery who transcends all religion. Eckhart scholar Hee-Sung Keel has these relevant words:

> Christianity is in serious crisis today . . . At the heart . . . is its popular but highly problematic concept of God as a personal being who is all too human to be credulous and who is believed to be omnipotent and yet seems so powerless to answer the host of perplexing questions we face in life and history. Christian theology, in my mind, has to reformulate its view of God in such a way that it mends the rupture between God and the world . . . and enables us to rediscover the sacred in the midst of our everyday life.[1]

Eckhart's mystical path directly addresses these issues by emphasizing our oneness with the mystery of God in daily life.

Basically, we think God is a supreme being. It is the way Christianity has packaged God, and it is the way our culture views God. God is a big cosmic being up there somewhere in the outer reaches of space, a kind of nice and gentle Zeus. This makes God one being among many beings. There are all sorts of examples of people treating God like a being, like a thing. I've heard God referred to as "Santa Claus" for grown-ups or an adult's imaginary friend. Wondering why there isn't scientific evidence for

---

1. Keel, *Meister Eckhart: An Asian Perspective*, 21.

God is to treat the divine reality as a thing. Not getting what we want from God—as though God granted wishes—is to treat God like a being.

We tend to see, relate to, and treat God as a thing for our use. We are guilty of reducing the unimaginable mystery to manageable proportions. We mold God into our image, so we can control our world. Meister Eckhart prays that God might free us of the God we manipulate to our own purposes. As Jon Sobrino says, "Jesus sees the de facto evil use of power rooted in the will to power—specifically in the power that tries to manipulate God."[2] When we treat God as a being or as a thing, we can control him (and in this case of mistaken identity, God is definitely male and white) and use him to legitimize our way of organizing the world. So, men in power can use the image of God as a Father to legitimize patriarchy. White men in power can turn God into an old white man and use their false image of God to support racism, sexism, and oppression of the poor.

In *Transforming Our Days*, theologian Richard Gaillardetz explains three consequences of understanding God as a being. First, we think God is out there somewhere, totally removed from our lives and our hearts. Second, God as a being means God has to compete for our love. Third, God as a being means we can only experience God in an episodic fashion.[3] If I only meet God in little episodes of my life—church services, prayer times, Bible reading—then it is but one commodity among others in my day. It will not likely change me, nor will this episodic spirituality change the world. Instead, the sharp divide between religious experience and everyday experience is made stronger. God, in effect, becomes wholly unrelated to daily life.

ALAN THE ATHEIST

Alan does not believe in God. He got turned off to religion through a variety of experiences. As a child his parents forced him to go to church. The minister relished telling the people how they would go to hell for all eternity if they did not accept every word in the Bible as literally true. A question formed in Alan's mind: how could a loving God condemn anyone to hell for all eternity? When he was in high school, his dad died in a car crash. At the funeral, one of his well-intentioned aunts tried to console him saying, "Al, God just wanted your ol' daddy back." Naturally, Alan felt angry with

2. Sobrino, *Christology at the Crossroads*, 121.

3. Gaillardetz, *Transforming Our Days*, 28–30.

this supposed God. He only chose unbelief, though, once he got to college and took a philosophy class. He connected with some atheist thinkers such as Frederick Nietzsche and Bertrand Russell.

Alan moved from doubting God's existence to flat out denying it. He returned home an avowed atheist, much to the ire of his mother. In fact, his unbelief and her belief caused such a rift between them that Alan's mother disowned him and has not spoken with him for years. Alan's atheism turned into downright hatred. This hatred, though, did not prevent him from falling in love with a woman named Angela, who was just plain indifferent to religion. They started a family and had three boys. They decided to raise their boys without any belief in God and without any relationship to Alan's mother.

Though an extreme case, I believe Alan's experience of religion and belief in God matches many others' experience. Alan labored under a terrible conception of God as well as both a conformist and negative style of Christianity. When the minister from his youth emphasized hell and blind faith in a literal understanding of the Bible, he both distorted Christian faith and ensured that intelligent people would walk away, never to return. Alan's well-meaning aunt represents conventional religion. Her trite saying in response to Alan's grief comes across as hurtful at worst and irrelevant at best. Then his mother makes it worse by disowning him simply because he does not share her belief. That is the kind of religion that hurts and even kills. Alan did what any sane person would. He walked away.

Meister Eckhart opposes conventional and bad religion. Instead, he focuses on a God whom Alan might be happy to believe in and commit his life to. Eckhart preaches the Gospel, radical and alluring, in his own key. With words, phrases, and images never used before, Eckhart shocks us out complacent, conformist, and often hateful religion. To Alan and all atheists Eckhart says, "God is not what you think." He presents them with a sort of "mystical atheism." To religious people like Alan's mother, aunt, and minister, Eckhart says, "Let go of your understanding of God and religion. It is hurting the world, and I have something phenomenally better." To people who are indifferent like Angela, Alan's wife, Eckhart says, "Indescribable joy can be yours if only you open your heart and mind." Eckhart has something to say to all of us.

The kind of God Alan experienced doesn't make sense to many people today. This "Zeus-like" god is so unbelievable and irrelevant to life that many turn away from faith and live in either unbelief or indifference. At this juncture, a problem arises. Our culture tends to force everyone into self-absorption. Through social media and consumerism, it is likely many of us will exhibit narcissistic traits. Because of this, the contemporary person, living in a world where there is little God-reference, gets thrown back on the self. We are saturated with self-reference. More precisely, our world drips with ego-reference. Such prevalent egocentricity does not bode well for our world. We desperately need a new way of seeing God, of seeing nothing but God. Meister Eckhart, faithful to the vision of Jesus, gives us a way to see God by entering the ground.

TRINITY

Who is this God with whom we are one in the ground? How does Eckhart present this God with whom our culture has such a problem? For Eckhart, God is Trinity and God is mystery. In neither case is God a supreme being. Even though God is Trinity, Eckhart maintains that our words and ideas do not capture who God really is. Hence, mystery is the all-encompassing reality when we talk about God, for God is beyond words, ideas, and even our very existence.

Though radical, Eckhart is still a Catholic Christian. He preaches the God who is Trinity. He preaches God as Father, Son, and Holy Spirit. Of course, he does so in his own incomparable way. As a brief sketch of his theology of the Trinity, I want to present three images he uses for the Trinity: boiling, laughter, and the birth.

Imagine a pot of water set to boil. As it starts to heat, it bubbles slightly. Then, it bubbles forcefully until the water is nearly exploding out of the pot. This is the image Eckhart uses to describe the inner life of the Trinity and how creation happens. He says God's inner life of Father, Son, and Holy Spirit is like the inner boiling of a pot of water. Each divine person's love for the other froths and cooks to make each person distinct yet fuse them in the oneness of God's nature. When God creates, this inner boiling life of the Trinity erupts like a pot of water boiling too long and shooting water onto a stove. Creation happens when the life of the Trinity boils over.[4] Boiling represents the Triune God as explosively powerful and not simply a static presence to be worshipped.

Charmingly, Eckhart describes the Trinity as God laughing at the divine self. He says, "Do you want to know what goes on in the core of the

4. McGinn, *The Mystical Thought of Meister Eckhart*, 72–74.

Trinity? I will tell you. In the core of the Trinity the Father laughs and gives birth to the Son. The Son laughs back at the Father and gives birth to the Spirit. The whole Trinity laughs and gives birth to us."[5] He also claims the joy arising from Father and Son laughing together produces the Holy Spirit. It gives one a sense that God takes great pleasure in being God, and maybe doesn't take the whole thing too seriously either.

A third metaphor Eckhart uses to describe the Trinity is one of the major symbols of his mysticism, the birth. Some scholars say Eckhart's whole point is that we give birth to the Word in our souls, which means that we experience a spiritual awakening. Birthing, though, also gives us a window into the life of the Trinity and how we are part of that life, too. Our birth is one with God the Father giving birth to the Son and the two persons breathing forth the Spirit. We wake up spiritually by the same explosive divine energy that makes up the Trinity.

God the Father through the Son and by the Holy Spirit brings us into the divine life. Eckhart makes this point in Sermon Four. He tells his congregation about how God so enjoys giving birth to the Son and that God doesn't want to do anything else! This delightful birthing then blossoms in the Holy Spirit. In this birthing and blossoming of Son and Spirit from the Father, God gives birth to the soul. There I am born as one and the same Son, Jesus Christ. Eckhart notes, quickly, that each of us is still different and distinct in our humanity; nevertheless we are each one and the same Christ. Thus, we enter the life of the Trinity through the Son, Jesus Christ.

So, the Trinity is centrally important to the Meister. Trinity is how God relates to us. In being the Son, we are one with God the Father through the Holy Spirit. In being the Son, we are identical with the Godhead in the ground. Jesus Christ is the place where we stand in relation to the Father and the Spirit is the bond of love connecting us to the Father from the place where we stand.

MYSTERY

Still, the doctrine of the Trinity, at least as we understand it, does not exhaust the reality of God. The divine reality transcends the whole of creation, all that exists. Meister Eckhart invites us into the divine mystery, the God beyond God, when he says our core desire is to go "into the simple ground, the silent desert, into which distinction never gazed, not the Father, nor

5. Fox, *Meditations with Meister Eckhart*, 129.

the Son, nor the Holy Spirit."[6] Eckhart also refers to the "Godhead," which transcends everything we know of God, everything we believe. God as mystery means God is unknown and transcendent. Much more than we can conceive, much more than we can experience, the divine reality cannot be captured in either word or feeling. God is incomprehensible. God is beyond being.

The preaching of the Meister constantly undercuts traditional belief and a common understanding of God. The term "Godhead" is but one of the many names Eckhart uses to represent the infinitely vast mystery of God. Along with "Godhead," words like "nothing" and "desert" form part of a central strategy of Eckhart's mysticism. This strategy is called "apophasis." This word means "unsaying." It is the theological strategy by which one uses language to show how language breaks down when we talk about God. This is a way that strips all names from God because God is beyond them all.

Now, Meister Eckhart is not splitting God. He is not saying there's this one God called Trinity and another God behind the Trinity. In Sermon Ten, Eckhart says that the distinction between Father, Son and Spirit comes from their oneness as a single Godhead. Their unity is their distinction in contrast to everything created, which is characterized by multiplicity. Eckhart is outlining a core principle: identical oneness differentiates. He reconciles oneness and difference, which he sees as essential to God. The divine nature is a dynamic paradox pulsating between absolute Oneness and Trinitarian persons. No distinction without indistinction. God is not one or the other. The more the persons of the Trinity are distinct, the more they are one and indistinct. Cyprian Smith, Benedictine monk and commentator on Meister Eckhart, describes this fundamental paradox in the mysticism of Meister Eckhart with a connection to our lives:

> God is everything yet nothing; distinct from creation, yet indistinct from it; there is a tension between action and contemplation, withdrawal and involvement, silence and speech, being and nothingness.[7]

Just as God is the paradoxical unity of infinite mystery and love overflowing as Trinity, our lives are the unity of contemplation and action. They are a paradoxical coincidence of solitude and deep engagement with the world. According to Eckhart, how God is with the world leads to how we are to be in the world.

6. Eckhart, *Meister Eckhart: The Essential Sermons*, 198.
7. Smith, *The Way of Paradox*, 27.

Through Son and Spirit, God the Father draws us back into the mystery of the divine identity. The Father is the source of the Trinity. The Son is the Word revealing the infinite mystery of the Godhead. The Holy Spirit is the love with which God loves us. God is both Trinity and Godhead. The Trinity is also the mystery of the God beyond God. Who we really are is tied to this divine mystery.

PRETENDING TO BE A KLUTZ

In high school I went on an interfaith pilgrimage to the Holy Land with a group of Jewish and Catholic teenagers. Two rabbis and a nun were our chaperones. We visited Jewish holy sites like the Western Wall as well as Christian holy sites like the church of the Holy Sepulcher which covers both the place of Jesus' crucifixion and his tomb. It was the experience of a lifetime.

I wanted to be liked, especially by the girls. So, I put on an act, one I thought people would find funny. I pretended to be a klutz, constantly falling, tripping, or otherwise "hurting myself." Only, it was all fake. I was not really accident prone, but that was the image I felt I needed to project because that's who I wanted to be. I'm not sure it would've occurred to me that I was being disingenuous. Of course, everyone saw through my act, and made fun of me for it. Still, once a few people on the trip got to know me beyond the act, they liked me as I was.

It was a stark contrast being in the places where Jesus walked while pretending to be someone else. Jesus was utterly authentic. He knew who he was. At that time, on that trip, I did not know who I was. I was so focused on myself and my needs (wanting to be liked, craving female attention) that I lost any real sense of identity. Eckhart, following Jesus, sees how we do not know who we are. We don't know we are one with God right here and right now. He believes our primary obstacle is the self or ego.

I didn't know who I was. We don't know who we are. Because we do not know who we really are, we invest our identity in everything under the sun. We think our identity is found in our ethnicity, our nationality, our religion, our gender, our politics, and our science to name just a few. In essence, we derive a sense of self from our thoughts, feelings, and experiences about all these things. We create a self because we do not know who we really are. This manufactured self is the problem. Spiritual teachers today call it the ego. Throughout his sermons and other writings, Meister Eckhart accurately describes the ego and its machinations.

THE "NOT" THAT SEPARATES

Throughout many of Meister Eckhart's sermons, delivered to laypeople, nuns, and priests in medieval Germany, the theme of the self and the obstacles it presents to knowing God within are constant. In Sermon 12, Eckhart says that anyone who wants to remain in God's love should be dead to the self and with it all created things. He is talking about our addiction to ego and the many attachments it creates.

I think, though, Eckhart cuts to the quick when he says that there is a "not" between two individuals. The not creates the difference between them and is the cause of discord. The problem with ego is that it suffers from the illusion that everything is separate. This illusion of separation is an inner problem. Eckhart names it the "not." I am not you. I am not God. There is something in me that is not in God. This "not" separates. It keeps me from God and others. The "not" appears whenever we say something like, "Thank God I'm not like him or her." "Not" equals opposition, comparison, and accusation. It is, in a word, judgment.

We create the ego when we do not know who we are. The ego functions by a process of separation. We falsely think we are not one with God. Because we feel separate from God, we focus exclusively on ourselves. The ego then separates itself further by investing things and thoughts with a sense of identity. The ego identifies with things, which really means identifying with thoughts. Our egos are about creating a false identity by being obsessed with the self's image, its maintenance, and its pleasure. In a word, the ego is utterly self-centered. In this state, we bolster this ego by setting it off from others. Eckhart says, "All creatures have a negation in themselves; one creature denies that it is the other creature."[8] One creature is not another creature.

One of the ways this works in daily life is when we try to elevate ourselves above others. We do and think things that make us feel superior. We use morality, culture, our intelligence, and even our relationships to make ourselves feel like we're better than everyone else. We try to separate ourselves out from the mass of humanity to feel special. We want to feel like

---

8. Eckhart, *Meister Eckhart: Teacher and Preacher*, 281.

we are above everyone else, because we know something they don't, have a lifestyle they don't, or believe something they don't.

We're always separating. We do it nationally and internationally. We separate ourselves from groups we consider beneath us or dangerous: I'm American and I'm good. He's Muslim and he's bad. We divide people into the good and the bad. This is a great lie: that there are some who are totally evil and some who are totally good. Everyone is a mix, despite the rare cases of psychosis, which prove the general rule. The problem is in us. We think we are separate.

WE JUDGE

Now, because we think we are separate, we judge. Of course, this is exactly what Jesus told us not to do. He says, "Stop judging and you will not be judged" (Luke 6:37). Judgment comprises complaining, comparing, and accusing. We might call this dynamic the judgment trap. It starts with complaining. We do it to make ourselves feel superior, because we know our egos are so fragile—precisely because they are not really who we are! We complain about people: what someone may have done to us, what someone thinks, or what others have done that we think is horrible. We complain about situations: circumstances that are intolerable to our sensibilities, situations that keep us from getting what we want, or experiences beyond our comfort zones. Again, we do this because we want to feel in control and better than the person or situation we are complaining about. Complaining keeps us imprisoned in our own little worlds of feeling like a victim and not taking responsibility for our own nonsense. Whenever we complain, we concoct a story about how we are right and someone else is wrong.

Complaining lies in the same camp as comparing. It's natural for us to compare ourselves to each other. We can't help but notice how others differ from us on a physical level. We get trapped, however, when we let comparisons define us and control us. It happens when we see a "perfect body" and feel shame about our own. It happens when we envy someone else because they're wealthier, more together, or happier in whatever way we define it. On the other hand, we can use the people and things in our lives to enhance our own self-image and make ourselves the envy of the block.

The judgment trap hardens into accusation. When we accuse, we think the other person is the problem. We think other people, situations, life itself are the problem. And so, we accuse everything and everyone. We think evil is over there, in the other. We do not recognize that we are the problem. Because we are blind to our own complicity in evil, we believe that the only response to evil is to squash it, destroy it, and make it go away. We deal with evil by killing it, blowing it up, or wiping it out. This has cast a shadow over every people. In fact, this often shows up in our movies.

The judgment trap is a feature of our thinking that results from the "not" that separates. We perceive the world as divided and we react accordingly. This normal mode of thinking often holds us back from realizing the truth of our oneness with the divine. Instead, we try to be distinct on our own terms, and this is our false identity. Our real identity, though, is found in nothing but God. Eckhart says our true self emerges from the ground, for in the ground there is nothing but God.

THE EXPLOSIVE METAPHOR OF THE GROUND[9]

Who we really are and what we have always been lies in the ground. Our souls ache for the unity found there. The mysticism of Meister Eckhart centers around the word "ground." It is an image exploding with meaning for Eckhart. By means of this metaphor, Eckhart shatters conventional and ultimately self-deceptive thinking about God and the human person. Through the word "ground" Eckhart subverts the normal relation between God and the human person.

Reflecting on it as a metaphor, "ground" connotes stability, rootedness in the earth, or just the earth. I think of a great oak tree with its roots sunk deep down into the soil, firmly rooted in the earth. The ground is, also, common to all people. Everyone walks around on the ground. Stability and commonality lie within the word ground. Eckhart builds on these meanings by suggesting that every person is rooted in God. He gives the word mystical meanings. The ground is mystical identity and nonduality, the mystery of the God beyond God, and specifically the ground of Christ.

Meister Eckhart preaches, "God's ground is my ground and my ground is God's ground."[10] God and the soul are both grounded in the same ground, which has no ground. For Eckhart, this is the identity of God and the soul. The ground symbolizes mystical identity, which is the original transcendent oneness at the root of all reality. The ground is a symbol of nonduality.

9. McGinn, *The Mystical Thought of Meister Eckhart*, 38.

10. Eckhart, *Meister Eckhart: The Essential Sermons*, 183.

It symbolizes the God beyond God which is identical with the deepest and most foundational reality of each and every one of us. The ground is our own *I Am*. In this infinite depth, everyone can say with the man born blind, "I am" (John 9:9). Eckhart thought scriptures like John 17:21 express this indistinct oneness: "that they may all be one, as you, Father, are in me and I in you, that they also may be in us."

The ground is not our inner psychological world of thoughts and feelings. All too often we find our identities there, in our mental and emotional experiences. That is not what Eckhart means with this metaphor. Eckhart is not talking about our psychological self. Instead, the ground is the reality from which all that is springs. It is Foundational Reality, the really real. As such, in the ground the human person can be said to be divine.

At one and the same time, the soul remains unique while also being utterly identical with the God beyond God in the ground. Perhaps the ground as a simple metaphor of the earth or the floor works best to show how we are one yet distinct? We all walk on the same earth yet each of us is obviously distinct. There can be fifteen-hundred people all walking on the same field in a park, for instance. Thus, we share different places in space and time, while having different histories, cultures, ethnicities, and religions. Still, we all share one planet. We all share one earth. We are all in the same position of space, circling the sun. Just so, all things share one ground. Everything is one in and everything emerges from the ground as a distinct something or someone. Psychologically, the human person is still distinct. In the ground, however, the human person is identically one with God. This should not cause us any alarm because it is God who safeguards our distinction.

Furthermore, the ground is the mystery of God beyond all things. It is the source of all existence. It points to the mystery of God as the reality with which we are always engaged each moment of our lives. The ground is the reality in which we live, move, and have our being (cf. Acts 17:28). It is that out of which we exist. This eternal depth, then, is pure mystery. As such, Eckhart often speaks of the ground as nothing, or as transcending the God who is Trinity. For instance, in Sermon 48, Eckhart describes the ground as a simple silence deeper than the Holy Trinity. It signifies the inexhaustible nature of God who is beyond all things, and even deeper than existence. The ground is the God beyond God.

Another metaphor that functions as a synonym to the ground also appears throughout Eckhart's sermons: the desert. It is a symbol of nakedness, barrenness, and nothingness. Even though Eckhart uses metaphor, nothing can be said literally about the ground, for it is the divine reality as one beyond all distinction. The soul must divest itself of distinction before entering this deep incomprehensible reality. Even God must get naked of distinction before entering the ground. God can't enter the ground in any mode but only in a divine nakedness, that is, without any of the attributes we normally give God. For, in the ground all is one.

Eckhart's teaching may sound revolutionary and perhaps even somewhat beyond orthodox Christianity. One might well ask, where is Jesus in all of this? For Eckhart, Jesus Christ is essential. We realize we are one with God in the ground through Jesus Christ. In fact, this one ground is specifically the ground of Jesus Christ. As the Word and the Second Person of the Blessed Trinity, Jesus Christ dwells in the ground of God. The human soul does, too. Truly, the human soul also dwells in Christ. The one ground of God and the human soul is the ground of Jesus Christ.

When we enter the ground, we identify with and then give birth to Christ. For the Meister, Jesus is crucial because in him God became human. Eckhart holds to an ancient view of why God became human in Jesus. It was not only to save us from our sins, but also to make us one with God, too. God became human that humans might become God. This might be Eckhart's central point about Jesus Christ. Eckhart sees Jesus Christ as the one who reveals the ground where both God and the human soul are one beyond all distinction. Jesus brings us the blessedness and infinite joy of the one ground.

NOT LIKE THE DMV

I walk into the Department of Motor Vehicles to renew my driver's license. Immediately, I notice how long the line is. The DMV is bursting with people. The line stretches outside and wraps around the parking lot. I sigh and feel forced to accept that this is going to take a while. So, I get in line and wait. After an hour in line, I get to a clerk at a desk only to discover this is one of several lines I will have to wait on. Curse words explode in my head. This could take all day! The clerk also informs me about all the paperwork I will have to fill out, that is, in addition to the paperwork I have brought with me. I text my wife to say, "I don't think I'm getting out of here until dinner."

The next few hours I spend waiting, filling out paperwork, and then talking to clerks about more paperwork and more waiting. My frustration grows and grows. I never want to come back to this God-awful place! The whole thing seems like a gigantic waste of time as well as the very definition of "red tape." After waiting in the next line, I must see another clerk who gives me something to fill out and take to yet another clerk who has a long line. I wonder if there's ever an end to this misery! I finally reach the last clerk and turn in my paperwork only to discover I missed the deadline and have to start all over again!

Of course, Meister Eckhart never had to tangle with the DMV. Still, he was a leader of the Dominicans and a priest. He knew bureaucracy. He knew the medieval German equivalent of "red tape." This makes his teaching on the ground so amazing. For, the teaching on the ground says that everyone, everywhere, has immediate access to God. No barriers, no strings attached, and no red tape come between us and God in the ground.

THE BENEFITS OF THE GROUND

The ground proclaims identity with God is available now, right here! Spiritual growth may take time, but we can also enjoy this divine identity right now. We can enter the ground anywhere and anytime because the ground is within us: "whoever would enter God's ground, His inmost part, must first enter his own ground, his inmost part."[11] Everyone and anyone has immediate access to identity with the ultimate mystery. This is incredible news. In fact, Eckhart is revealing his deep connection to the Gospel through the image of the ground: there is nothing we have to do to get God because God is always and forever one with us, right here and right now! Jesus reveals this very God who is equally accessible and inherently connected to us.

There are no hoops to jump through to get God to love me. The ground tells us there are no requirements for oneness with God. Sinner and saint have equal access to the ground. There is nothing to do and there is nothing in the way of oneness with God. There is no form to fill out, no certificate to get, and no red tape. Oneness with God, for Meister Eckhart, is and will always be free and lacking in any paperwork. Our only problem is we don't know it because we are so addicted to the ego.

To enter the ground is to see reality as it is. When we see in this way, Eckhart assures us nothing is wasted. At times I can feel like my time is wasted, especially when I slump down in front of the television or when I do something selfish. Eckhart reminds me nothing is wasted when I turn

11. Eckhart, *The Complete Mystical Works of Meister Eckhart*, 251.

within and enter the ground. Everything is restored. Everything is used in my favor, even if we might be inclined to think we wasted our lives in sin and unresolved pain. God will use everything for our transformation, even our weakness, failure, sin, and suffering. Eckhart preaches in Sermon Five-b that if we only turn away from self and toward God for a single moment, then we are free, and whatever we lost due to selfishness is restored.

To know this core truth of the ground is to know joy. Meister Eckhart says, "all our perfection and all our bliss depends on our traversing and transcending all creatureliness, all being and getting into the ground that is groundless."[12] All our bliss lies in the ground because in the ground there is only the joy of the God beyond God. I'm not talking about happiness as an emotional high. Rather, I am talking about transcendent and ultimate joy, which is joy in the reality of one's own being. Other forms of happiness eventually disappoint because they don't last. The joy of the ground, on the other hand, is constant. A contemporary Dominican, Fr. Timothy Radcliffe, describes this divine joy well:

> This joy is not an emotion of God, a sunny, divine feeling. It is God's being. It is the 'I am' of the burning bush that Moses encountered in the wilderness . . . Because this delight is God's very being, then we cannot define it or understand it for . . . we cannot understand what it is for God to be God."[13]

God rejoices in God as God. God delights in each one of us as we are, too. Upon entering the ground, we realize that God's delight in the holy mystery of the God beyond God is identical with God's delight in the soul, for in the ground we are indescribably one with the God beyond God. In the ground, we inhabit, take as our own, and realize the very same delicious joy God has in being God.

GOING WITHIN TO EXPERIENCE THE GROUND

At the end of Sermon Five-b, Eckhart prays that we all may possess the truth within and without medium or distinction. His prayer sums up the thrust of our chapter on the ground and our identity: go within to experience the indistinct blessedness of the ground. When we stay on the surface of life and play the ego game, happiness eludes us. We remain ignorant

12. Eckhart, *The Complete Mystical Works of Meister Eckhart*, 400.
13. Radcliffe, *What is the Point of Being a Christian?*, 55.

of *who we really are* as long as we are caught in the grip of judgment and "the not." The illusion of being separate from everything reigns. Eckhart is luring us away from this illusion to enter the one ground, which is the dynamic unity between God and the self. This ground identity and its realization are vital for Eckhart.

At the core of discipleship is following Jesus into oneness: "The Father and I are one" (John 10:30). We are already one with God, but we have not yet fully integrated this deepest dimension of our identity with the rest of our lives. We are always and forever rooted in God. The spiritual journey is a matter of allowing what is most real about us—identity with God— to become real in our lives. It is about letting our inner divine identity to emerge into consciousness. Each of us is identically one with God in the ground. All the Meister's sermons invite us to dive into the one ground and realize our own divine identity. Eckhart wants to enlighten us about this one ground. He is proclaiming a wonderful truth: You don't need to do anything to achieve oneness with God. You are already one with God. But you don't know it because of all your attachments, false beliefs, illusions, blindnesses, resistances, and thinking. This is a mystical path of removing all that blocks our realizing that, in the ground, we are one with God. Even more, in the ground, there is nothing but God. My identity is found in nothing but God.

REFLECTION QUESTIONS

1. Are you familiar with the judgmental God presented to Alan the atheist? How has God been presented to you? Is this God someone you want to know?

2. How do you see yourself? What is your self-image?

3. What, typically, do you complain about? What does that tell you about your ego?

4. What keeps you on the surface of life? What distracts you from the one ground?

2

Letting Go into God

ONE OF THE BEST scenes in all of the *Star Wars* movies occurs in the very first one, *A New Hope*. The rebels are trapped on the fourth moon of Yavin as the dreaded Death Star closes in on them. They cook up a plan to send in one-man star fighters to take out the moon-sized space station by launching photon torpedoes into an exhaust portal only two meters wide. All the pilots groan and seem to assume such a shot is impossible. Luke Skywalker, though, leans over to his friend and boasts, "But it's not impossible. I used to bullseye womp rats in my T16 back home, they're not much bigger than two meters." The comment suggests Luke has a great deal of confidence in his own abilities. However, once Luke gets the chance to take the shot, the spirit of his teacher, Obi-Wan Kenobi, tells Luke, "Use the Force, Luke. Let go, Luke." Then, Obi-Wan says, "Luke, trust me." Skywalker had already turned on his targeting computer, suggesting he could take this shot on his own. After hearing Obi-Wan, though, Luke switches off his targeting computer and chooses to turn himself over to the Force. He decides to trust the Force and to let go of his way of doing things. He then makes the shot, destroys the Death Star, and saves the rebels from certain doom. The whole movie pivots on Luke's decision to surrender to the Force. It is a vivid depiction of the power of letting go.

WHAT IS DETACHMENT?

Meister Eckhart advises us to take his mystical path by practicing letting go, which he calls detachment. It is a constant theme in his sermons. For example, in Sermon 53, Eckhart tells his congregation he is used to speaking about detachment, which means being free of ego. The German word he uses for "detachment," *abegescheidenheit*, is translated literally as the process of "cutting off, or away" all attachments.[1] Detachment cuts off all the attachments that have separated us from our oneness with God. By detachment we enter the ground where we are fully one with God.

For Meister Eckhart, we follow Jesus by practicing detachment. Eckhart interprets Jesus' teaching, "Whoever wishes to come after me must deny himself, take up his cross, and follow me" (Mark 8:34)" to mean detachment. He tends to focus less on the historical facts of the life of Jesus as much as the spiritual attitudes Jesus wants us to imitate. Yet, Eckhart clearly identifies detachment with the cross. He says, "God died so that I might die to the whole world and to all created things."[2] We follow Christ Crucified, then, by detaching and not by rigorous penances and the multiplication of religious activities.

Of course, once we try to detach from anything in our lives, we find out how hard it is. We need help. Eckhart says God initiates, sustains, and completes the process of detachment by a breakthrough. This is another major theme of Eckhart's mysticism. With God's help, we break through to the one ground and realize divine-human unity, which Eckhart also calls the birth of the Word in the soul. This is Eckhart's way of describing the process of transformation that Jesus calls being born again (John 3:3). Detachment and the breakthrough, then, mean letting go of images, of all created things, and even letting go of ideas of God. God's grace enables the soul to break through identification with a separate self and an attachment to a separate God. The breakthrough is God's work of uncovering our divine identity via a thorough detachment. We will explore detachment and the breakthrough in this chapter.

To detach is to enter the ground. To detach is to uncover our oneness with God. As Eckhart says in Sermon 71, we will only come to see that there is nothing but God through a practice of nothingness or not tying my identity to anything at all. Still, how do we detach? What does detachment mean?

Detachment for Eckhart is prayer: "detachment makes me receptive of nothing but God."[3] Specifically, it is contemplative prayer. We learn to

1. McGinn, *The Mystical Thought of Meister Eckhart*, 143.

2. Eckhart, *Meister Eckhart: Teacher and Preacher*, 289.

3. Eckhart, *The Pocket Meister Eckhart*, 104.

let go as we rest in God in silence. Thomas Keating calls it "a state of no-thinking."[4] This is the heart of detachment for Eckhart. It is a state of mind in which we are not thinking yet fully centered on nothing but God. The last phrase, namely "centered on nothing but God," sounds like we're thinking about God. That is not the case. We are silently resting in God without thinking. Keating describes it well: "Let thoughts come, let them go. No annoyance, no expectation."[5] We let thoughts pass through us as we stay rooted in the presence of God by remaining silent within.

The practice becomes clearer as we delve into Eckhart's teaching on detachment. He describes it in many ways, but three stand out. They are: paying attention to God, *gelassenheit* (releasing), and subtraction. Each informs an understanding of Eckhart's idea of detachment as letting go into God.

PAYING ATTENTION TO GOD

Detachment is like my decision to turn away from a desire to watch television in order to play with my daughter. I turn my attention *away from* the television and simultaneously turn my attention *to* my daughter. Detachment occurs when we turn away from paying attention to self, and we turn towards paying attention to God in the present moment. We do not pay attention to God like all the people and objects in our lives, for God is God and not just another entity in the universe. Paying attention to God is simply to be present in the now in faith.

Biblically, detachment is based on the first commandment. To give our attention to God here and now is to give God the priority of being God. It is to let God be God. In Exodus, God tells Moses:

> I am the Lord your God . . . You shall not have no other gods besides me. You shall not make for yourself an idol or a likeness of anything in the heavens above or on the earth below or in the waters beneath the earth; you shall not bow down before them or serve them" (Exodus 20:2–5).

Only God is God, and nothing else. Therefore, we worship nothing but God. If we worship anything else, those are idols. We are giving them attention over and above God. Idols preoccupy us and cause us to lose our freedom,

4. Keating, *Open Mind, Open Heart*, 92.
5. Keating, *Open Mind, Open Heart*, 62.

peace, and joy. God alone is our freedom, peace, and joy. Thus, detachment rests securely on the foundation of the first commandment to worship, or pay attention to, nothing but God. Jesus builds on the first commandment when he tells his followers: "everyone of you who does not renounce all his possessions cannot be my disciple" (Luke 14:33).

About prayer, Eckhart advises sinking into the divine nothingness in whom we lose self-awareness. This is, in fact, attention-less attention or pure attention. Contemporary teachers of contemplative practice emphasize that one focuses on nothing in prayer, for God is not an object on which one can focus. Prayer means transcending the self, and only God can help with this. Such is the process of detachment: transcending the self by paying attention to God and relaxing our hold on attachments. In short, living a detached life means living a holy life. It means paying attention to nothing but God.

GELASSENHEIT

Eckhart tends to use words like detachment, renunciation, and abandonment when he preaches about the need to let go. He also uses words that are gentler. Words like release, resign, and sink appear in his sermons often. Another one of these words is *gelassenheit*, which means "releasement." This word helps us understand what Eckhart means by detachment. Again, translated from the original German, *gelassenheit* means a state of releasement. I think we might profitably understand this word to mean "relaxing into God." I relax the tight grip I have on all the things I think will give me happiness. I get so uptight, overprotective, and invested in the things I think I need to be happy. Eckhart is saying, "relax." I release my hold on these things, for they won't give me lasting happiness. I take it easy and unhook myself from these attachments. I don't get so worked up about them. I attend to the divine presence within.

Detachment, then, means releasing our grip and relaxing our efforts to get the thing we think we need. Relaxing our grip communicates the relief and relaxation that come from letting go. In Sermon 59, Eckhart claims that self-denial and detachment relieve suffering and provide joy. Typically, when we do not get the things we think we need to be happy, we experience some form of suffering. Detachment releases us from tying our happiness to the things we think we need so that we can find our happiness in God.

Detachment can be illustrated by looking at acupuncture. It mixes two disparate feelings: pain and relaxation. My acupuncturist does acupressure on my head while there are needles in my belly, fingers, feet, and toes. It is not tremendously painful, but it does hurt. Additionally, she will put moxa (a dried plant) on my torso and back, and then light it on fire. Sometimes I barely feel it, and other times it burns badly! Still, it is weirdly relaxing. The end of the therapy nears as she places needles in my back and then pinches my shoulders and digs a needle into the muscles of my shoulder. She is loosening the knots in my shoulder muscles. It hurts, but it is fantastic. The needles untie muscular knots deep in my shoulder and it is extremely relaxing. I always leave the acupuncturist stress-free and loose.

Detachment works like acupuncture. It sometimes does hurt to surrender the thing I love, which is the thing I believe will satisfy me. It can be as objectively trivial as turning off the television or not plugging in my iPhone and as objectively hard as an alcoholic not drinking. Still, detachment relaxes my tightly held grip on my own egoic happiness projects. Letting go releases my muscular knot of attachment, and is, therefore, relaxing.

SUBTRACTION

The root meaning of detachment in Middle High German is "cutting off," so the idea of removing something is critical to practicing detachment. In this regard, Meister Eckhart says, "God is not found in the soul by adding anything, but by a process of subtraction."[6] In this consumer culture, we tend to think the more we do, the better, and the more we have, the better. I think we unconsciously apply this perspective to the spiritual life. We presume that doing more religious things, even going to church more often, automatically put us in God's good graces. Eckhart vigorously denounced this consumer mind throughout his writings, and we will look more closely at it in chapter 6. Instead of adding things to our lives, the Meister would tell us not to acquire more things, even if they are spiritual, but to drop all the things we think we need.

God is found through subtraction. We have to peel off and strip away layers of falsehood, misperception, attachment, narrow-mindedness, and prejudiced thinking to awaken. The thing to subtract is thinking. We identify with our thinking, believing that is who we really are. If one removes this attachment to thinking, the ground identity emerges. Dropping

6. Fox, *Passion for Creation*, 183.

thinking, wanting, and our emotional reactions necessitates a reduction to a clear intention for God. Eckhart teaches that this intention must be simple so that we seek nothing in addition to God and nothing except God. The soul must subtract everything else.

Subtraction gets to the heart of detachment for Eckhart, for the word *abegescheidenheit* means "cutting off." Detachment is a removal, a peeling away of the false skins hiding the divine nothing within us. Charlotte Radler, a contemporary Eckhart scholar, comments, "a detached human being removes layer after layer of its constructed pseudo-self until it uncovers the true core of itself."[7] To detach is to subtract all the layers of ego to discover God. Eckhart proclaims, "Now put aside 'this' and 'that,' and what remains is nothing but God."[8] Sometimes while preaching, Eckhart uses the image of clothing to communicate this message. For instance, we detach as we take off God's coat—our ideas of God—to see the bare divine nature.

LETTING GO INTO GOD

"Letting go" is a good synonym for Eckhart's detachment as long as we understand detachment has a target for Meister Eckhart. Notice how Luke lets go and trusts the Force. His letting go had a direction. Such is the case with Meister Eckhart's teaching. For him detachment is all about nothing but God. We could call Eckhart's practice of detachment, "letting go into God." We let go into nothing but God. Hence, detachment implies prayer or centering our hearts on God alone. It is a process of dis-identifying from everything we think we are, the self-conceptions that cause us to forget our oneness with God in the ground. Keating teaches that "detachment is the goal of self-denial . . . The false self is a monumental illusion, a load of habitual thinking patterns and emotional routines that are stored in the brain and nervous system."[9] We shed our false identities by abiding in the holy mystery of God by being no distinct thing, that is, by not letting our identities set us off from others. We're too obsessed with being special and standing out. We think this is what life is about, but it's just an ego need to feel superior. Eckhart encourages us to become nobody, pure nothing.

7. Radler, "Losing the Self," 113.

8. Eckhart, *The Complete Mystical Works of Meister Eckhart*, 389.

9. Keating, *Open Mind, Open Heart*, 15.

We let go to realize nothing but God, to center on God alone. As Eckhart says, "detachment makes me receptive of nothing but God."[10] Detachment has one purpose: God. Freedom and joy, infinite beatitude and love, spring up from detachment, but its focus is exclusively on God and not on all our preoccupying attachments. Eckhart's detachment fosters a letting go of attachments and a fundamental enjoyment of God. We let go into nothing but God. It is prayer, pure and simple.

A scene from the end of the film *Indiana Jones and the Last Crusade* summarizes this brief presentation of detachment according to Meister Eckhart. In this scene, Indiana Jones struggles to hold on to the beautiful Austrian professor, Elsa Schneider. She is dangling over a crevasse that has opened up in a temple in the Middle East. As she holds on to Indiana Jones for dear life, she stretches out to get the object she and Indiana have been seeking for the whole of their journey: The Holy Grail, the cup Jesus drank from at the Last Supper. It is resting on a small cliff just out of reach. Moments before, Jones had used the cup to save his own father's life. It is a powerful object, and Elsa greatly desires it. As she reaches for it, Indiana can't hold on to her. She slips out of his grasp and plummets to her doom. Simultaneously, Jones falls into the crevasse and his dad catches him. Like Elsa, Indiana stretches out to try to grab the Holy Grail. He tells his dad, "I can get it. I can almost reach it, Dad." Of course, his other hand begins to slip out of his dad's grip. Then, his father says, "Indiana, Indiana, let it go." Jones turns to face his dad, gives him his other hand, and his dad pulls him to safety.

Indiana Jones had to relax his mental grip on possessing the Holy Grail, an obsession that would have killed him. If he had been focused on getting it for but a few more seconds, he would have slipped through his father's hands and fallen to his death like the beautiful Austrian professor. Also, notice how Jones turns his gaze away from the cup and towards his dad. He listens to his dad and lets it go. Indiana Jones has to release his mental grip on the Grail, and he turns his attention to his dad. He lets go of himself in the process. Just so, we let go or detach by releasing our mental grip on some glittery object of supposed happiness and turn our attention to God within. To do so is to transcend the self and enter into God's own life.

10. Eckhart, *The Pocket Meister Eckhart*, 104.

WHAT PREOCCUPIES US

If detachment as letting go into God is fundamentally about paying attention to God, we need to examine what we tend to give our attention to instead of God. Eckhart recognizes how detachment "demands hard work and great dedication and a clear perception of our inner life and an alert, true, thoughtful and authentic knowledge of what the mind is turned towards in the midst of people and things."[11] Eckhart names a few of these obstacles, which I think provide opportunities to bring detachment into our everyday lives. He talks about them in Sermon 12. After reviewing this sermon below, we will summarize his teaching on attachments by looking at our attachment to thinking as Eckhart describes it at the end of Sermon One.

In Sermon 12, Meister Eckhart observes that there are three major obstacles to realizing we are one with God: temporality, multiplicity, and corporality. These three dimensions of consciousness consume our attention. We are time conscious (temporality), distraction conscious (multiplicity), and body conscious (corporality). We get so preoccupied with these mindsets that we lose awareness of God. These three hindrances are to some extent the products of a materialist culture. Our culture tells us there is nothing beyond this life: no God, no soul, and no afterlife exist. With what, then, are we left? We are left with time, our bodies, and whatever amusements or anxieties we can concoct to distract us from the always approaching specter of death. For those walking the mystical path of nothing but God, however, temporality, multiplicity, and corporality are not ends in themselves but opportunities to sink ever-more deeply into God.

Temporality is when we are preoccupied with time. We get trapped by the past and by the future. Lacking a focus on the God within, we easily slip into time consciousness. This can take both positive and negative forms. There is worrying about the future or eagerly awaiting something. There is regretting the past and feeling ashamed or guilty. There is also pride, fondness, and nostalgia concerning the past. All are features of time consciousness. Now, none of these are absolute in themselves, but we make them absolute by focusing on them so much. It is no real problem to remember the past or to project to the future. Life in the world requires it. Eckhart, though, is talking about how time can take center stage in our minds and even control us. This results in never living in the present moment.

11. Eckhart, *Meister Eckhart: Selected Writings*, 11.

An example of temporality is how we get ready for work in the morning. I don't think it is too much of a generalization to say that getting to work on time is a major priority for most of us. Everything else may revolve around this priority: breakfast may need to be on the go, goodbyes to our loved ones may not happen, and our driving can go from normal to unsafe all-too-quickly. We get so focused on the future, worried about making it to work on time and what might happen if we do not show up on time, that we miss the present moment.

Multiplicity might be an apt name for our twenty-first century globalized culture. Multiplicity is Meister Eckhart's word for distraction. We can also call it busy-ness. Multiplicity means we are so riveted by other things—our thoughts, our feelings, other people and our relationship to them, work issues, entertainment—that we are totally lost in these many things. Life is busy! How many things do we have on our "to-do" lists? What chores need doing? When do I have to pick up the kids? Will I have time to cook dinner? Did I call that person back? Did my check bounce? Will I beat the traffic? Sometimes, it seems like the more we get done, the more hectic life gets. No wonder stress is a big health concern.

The mind shaped by multiplicity fosters a grotesque triviality at the heart of our lives. Our lives circle, maddeningly, I think, around the internet, television and movies, and shopping. We are never concerned about the deeper things of life, the sacred things. Instead, we flit from television show to website, from one Instagram pic to the next. This happens via our extra appendage: our smart phones. We carry this ultimate distraction all over the place. Multiplicity is a consistent and definitive preoccupation.

As I wait in line at the grocery store, I look at the covers of half a dozen magazines. On each and every cover is a beautiful person: perfect complexion, svelte body, and gorgeous face. It is as if the magazines are telling me, "This is what men and women should look like. Instead they look like you." My thoughts go to my weight and to the unequal features that crop up all over my body. I wonder if I will ever go to the gym or eat right. I end up feeling bad about myself because I do not look like the guy on the cover of *GQ*. This is body consciousness, which Meister Eckhart names "corporality." It's an all-too-common experience of becoming self-conscious because of our bodies. Frequently, this produces shame. Of course, our culture does precious little to alleviate such shame. In fact, there are times we shame other people's bodies to make ourselves feel better.

Corporality means we are totally occupied and caught up with the physical self. We cannot see that there is more to life than the empirical and the physical. This might be the ultimate consequence of materialism, that is, of the belief that this is all there is. But, too many of us do not treat our bodies with any reverence or respect. Most of us, at some point, have allowed our concern for body image and appearance—"corporality" in Eckhart's terms—to crowd out any awareness of our oneness with God.

ECKHART'S TABLE TALKS

For a time, Meister Eckhart was the head friar, or what they call the prior, at the Dominican house in his hometown of Erfurt. He helped to train the young Dominicans, who were probably in their teens. In the evening, Eckhart would give them some basic teaching about the Gospel path. These are his "Talks of Instruction" or "Counsels of Discernment." We can call them "Table Talks" because he gave spiritual teaching to the young Dominican friars over a meal.

A core theme of these table talks is the self. He emphasizes the self as the main problem in the spiritual life. This is the main thing the mind is turned towards in daily life. In his third talk, "On undetached people who are full of self-will," Eckhart says, "Examine yourself, and wherever you find yourself, then take leave of yourself. This is the best way of all."[12] For the Meister, self is the core obstacle we face, and letting it go is the best path to follow.

Eckhart notes how so many novices complain that they will never become holy unless they can go to a monastery or live like a hermit. He diagnoses the issue with sage brevity: "The lack of peace that you feel can only come from your own self-will."[13] Their complaining reveals to the Meister how self-obsessed they are. The young Dominicans do not display a focus on God but only on how they wish they were different. Eckhart assures them that they will never know rest unless they give up the self.

If the young Dominicans in Eckhart's care were making holiness an ego project, then perhaps young people today can be forgiven for making social media an ego project? Our social media often reveal a huge amount of ego. Social media can create the conditions in which self-obsession grows, festers, and even becomes the normal way people interact. Social

12. Eckhart, *Meister Eckhart: Selected Writings*, 7.
13. Eckhart, *Meister Eckhart: Selected Writings*, 5.

media can be used for good, so my reflections are not absolute. Still, the ego sees a great opportunity for self-aggrandizement in social media. Whether it's Facebook, Twitter, Instagram, or Snapchat, social media allow us to project and cultivate an image of ourselves to the world. This is problematic because this self is not real.

The ego craves attention. Social media provide the platforms for the ego to promote itself and draw attention to itself. Again, social media can be used for good. My wife regularly posts pictures of my daughters so family in New York, South Carolina, Colorado, South Dakota, California, Florida, and even Costa Rica can feel connected to us. Perhaps, though, a need to be known takes over when I can't resist posting to Facebook, when I can't stop tweeting out what I am doing, or when I relish taking selfies every moment possible?

A WORD FROM THE MEISTER

In observing the young Dominicans and throughout his preaching, Eckhart seems to have accurately located the source of human misery: the ego. He may not use the word "ego," but he does have a word approximating our contemporary spiritual vocabulary. Eckhart's word for ego is *eigenschaft*. This is a medieval German word meaning possessiveness and self-reference.

Eigenschaft as possessiveness means clinging and grasping. The ego puts what it wants in a vice grip. The possessiveness of *eigenschaft* is the avid pursuit of what I think I need to be fulfilled and holding on to it for dear life. This does not apply solely to sports cars or high-definition televisions, but also to relationships and ways of living. I can cling to my way of doing things whether or not it's doing me harm. It is the attitude of doing what I want when I want. It is the clinging instinct in us that seeks to gain control, affection, and security above all else and on its own terms. Our ultimate possession is our homemade identity.

Essentially, as scholar Kurt Flasch writes, "'Eigenschaft' (property) is self-reference."[14] Self-reference is what the ego does; it is what the ego is. Everything has to be about me for the ego. Everything revolves around me. It's narcissism, pure and simple. We all suffer from the narcissistic ego. Rather than being the psychological diagnosis of narcissism as a personality disorder, Eckhart is teaching us about the way our consciousness works at an immature level. *Eigenschaft* refers everything in life to itself. *Eigenschaft*

14. Flasch, *Meister Eckhart: Philosopher of Christianity*, 54.

functions like a filter that sifts daily experience and only takes in what is relevant to me and my self-aggrandizement. Because we are paying so much attention to ourselves, we never pay attention to God. We identify with *eigenschaft* and forget we are one with God. *Eigenschaft* causes us to lose conscious connection to the one ground.

OUR ATTACHMENT TO THINKING

As we have seen, Eckhart names a few obstacles throughout his sermons, yet it seems to me he is more specific about these obstacles in Sermon One, where he likens the soul to a temple. He then preaches:

> If someone else but Jesus alone speaks in the temple (that is, the soul), then Jesus keeps silent as though he were not at home. And he is not at home in the soul then because it has other guests with whom it is conversing. But if Jesus is to speak in the soul, it must be alone and must itself remain silent if it is to hear Jesus speak.[15]

In this quote, Eckhart lays out our attachment to thinking. The ego separates itself from oneness with God by investing thoughts with a sense of identity.

Eckhart uses the temple as a metaphor for the soul, and the soul for Eckhart is the seat of consciousness. Because there are "strange guests" speaking in this temple, Jesus the Divine Word remains silent. He will not speak the divine nature—Eckhart's biblical symbol for realizing oneness with God—unless these "strange guests" are silent. These "strange guests" are interior voices. We all have these voices in our heads. One voice is *eigenschaft*, which tries to find ways to make the ego unique and different. Another voice is the merchant mind, rummaging around our minds until we go shop. Still another voice could be temporality, multiplicity, or corporality. The point is these voices in the temple are our thoughts. All the obstacles Eckhart names in his sermons are first thoughts in our minds. In this passage from Sermon One Eckhart is saying we need to silence these thoughts to listen to Jesus. In other words, we need to detach from our thinking.

These strange guests represent the interior dialogue, that conversation we carry on in our heads twenty-four hours a day. The ego talks to itself and its voices are manifestations of the obstacles Eckhart mentions. These inner

15. Eckhart, *Meister Eckhart: Teacher and Preacher*, 242.

voices prevent us from hearing Jesus. It is like flitting from guest to guest at a party you throw and not at all stopping to listen to your spouse who has something important to share with you. Eckhart has a quite astute point here: thinking hides our oneness with God.

Because of our thinking, we do not realize we're swimming in God. Martin Laird, a modern Augustinian friar and contemplative teacher, expresses this well:

> The reason for our ignorance of the most obvious and simplest of facts about our spiritual life is the constant inner noise and chatter that creates and sustains the illusion of being separate from God . . . Our culture for the most part trains us to keep our attention riveted to this surface noise, which in turn maintains the illusion of God as a distant object for which we must seek as for something we are convinced we lack.[16]

Thinking creates and maintains the illusion that you and I are separate from God.

We are attached to thinking. This may be the root attachment, and the place to start practicing detachment. The more we listen to the "strange guests" in our soul, our thoughts, the more we become fragmented and dysfunctional. All too often these strange guests, this inner noise, is incredibly negative and even destructive. Spiritual teachers the world over insist this thinking quickly becomes an addiction. All the spiritual obstacles we have examined are a complex of thoughts and feelings with which we identify.

In Sermon Two, Meister Eckhart calls the human soul to be "as free of all images as when he was nothing."[17] Here "images" equals "thoughts." Still, how can we be that free of thinking? Eckhart says that even if he knew all the images and was full of thinking but did not *cling* to thinking, he would be as free as he was when he was nothing. He invites us to be nonpossessive regarding our thinking. Both Eckhart and Laird are getting to the same point. Our identification with thinking is the root problem. Letting go of our attachment to thinking, then, lies at the heart of the practice of detachment.

---

16. Laird, *Sunlit Absence*, 2.

17. Eckhart, *Meister Eckhart: The Essential Sermons*, 177.

HOW TO DETACH

Detachment means centering on nothing but God. But centering does not mean merely "thinking" about God all the time. It is more profound than that. As we have seen, we tend to center on anything and everything but God. Our attachments preoccupy us. We pay attention to them and not to God, with whom we are one in the ground. We will never know our ground identity, our Christ nature, unless we turn our attention away from all the things to which we are attached. "The less we turn our aims or attention to anything other than God, and in so far as we look to nothing outward, so we are transformed in the Son . . ."[18] To detach means to stop paying attention to attachments and to pay attention to God. We need to let go into God. I have found three practical hints in the Meister's sermons for practicing detachment. They are: intention, is-ness, and nothingness. We shall briefly describe each.

First, intention for Eckhart means seeking and delighting in God alone. Eckhart teaches us to intend nothing but God. The soul settles for nothing less than God as God is in Godself. Therefore, we are to set our hearts on God alone. In Counsel Six, Eckhart says, "let our intention be purely and only for God."[19] Practically speaking, we simply set an intention: God. We can do it by saying a prayer, breathing, or reciting, "You alone, O God," for instance. The challenge is to set our intention at the beginning of the day and return to it all throughout the day.

Second, the Meister says, "God's is-ness is my is-ness."[20] Eckhart is saying we let go into God through *what is*. *What is* is now. To accept *what is* means to accept the content of the present moment, and to accept the divine is-ness present eternally in the now. The eternal is accessed through the now, meaning the present moment. Instead of obsessively pouring over our past or future, we are to be fully here and in the now. Sometimes we will feel like we cannot be present. All we need in that moment is the willingness to be present. In speaking of detachment, the Meister says, "All that it wants is to be."[21] *To be*, here and now, is to let go into God.

Third, Eckhart says to be nothing and nobody. In Sermon 52, he invites us to will nothing, know nothing, and have nothing. We allow our

18. Eckhart, *The Complete Mystical Works of Meister Eckhart*, 240–41.

19. Eckhart, *Meister Eckhart: The Essential Sermons*, 252.

20. Eckhart, *Meister Eckhart: The Essential Sermons*, 187.

21. Eckhart, *Meister Eckhart: The Essential Sermons*, 287.

interior world to be reduced to nothing. Thoughts will always be in our heads. We just stop paying attention to them and let them leave our interior world. Eckhart's practice of nothingness is roughly equivalent to what Keating calls interior silence: "By interior silence we refer primarily to a state in which we do not become *attached* to the thoughts as they go by."[22] In the state of interior silence and stillness, there is no attachment to anything at all, and that includes both our self-image and our image of God.

Detachment, like Centering Prayer of Christian Meditation, is a practice of letting the internal dialogue dissolve into silence. We become nothing because seeking God is not like seeking any-*thing* in the world. God is not a being or a thing in the world. God is the ground of existence, the holy mystery from which everything comes and to which everything returns. So, our desire for God needs to focus on God properly, and not on God as one more thing. God is not a thing; God transcends everything. Therefore, we "sink down, out of 'something' into 'nothing.'"[23] There must be an interior nothingness, a letting go, and a silencing of all mental activity and thinking to discover the divine nothing.

To make this as clear and as practical as possible, Eckhart teaches us to practice detachment first by praying contemplatively, then by taking this contemplative mindset into the world. We intend God alone, consent to God within us, root ourselves in the present moment, and ignore our thinking. For many, the best way to facilitate this movement into inner nothingness happens via a holy word, breathing, or a sacred image. These are all traditional Christian contemplative means to inhabit the state of mind in which we are centered on nothing but God. So, it is best to start with a contemplative prayer practice, then use the means—a word, breathing, an image—as a bridge into everyday living. If we choose, for instance, a word, then that word symbolizes our delight in God alone. It helps us to shrug off preoccupation with past and future. The prayer word leads us into interior nothingness, where we are not drawn into inner mental self-talk. While a relatively simple practice, the challenge is to remain in this state of delighting in God in the now and beyond thinking. It is a practice that leads to a state of mind.

22. Keating, *Open Mind, Open Heart*, 43.
23. Eckhart, *Meister Eckhart: The Essential Sermons*, 208.

LETTING GO: A STATE OF MIND

Joel Harrington, expert on medieval German history, translates *gelassenheit* as "letting-go-ness."[24] This is a good description of detachment. "Letting-go-ness" is a state of mind. Eckhart calls it "the right state of mind."[25] This tells us that detachment is not necessarily a once-for-all choice, but a constant letting go and letting be. As a state of mind, it is silent, pure, and inherently nothing. Our minds, though, are filled with things. Winston Churchill was reported to have said, "Maturing is realizing how many things don't require your comment." Eckhart might quip in reply, "Nothing needs our comment!" Letting-go-ness is the state in which one ignores the ego and its commentary.

Eckhart describes detachment with a wonderful image, "true detachment is nothing else than for the spirit to stand as immovable against whatever may chance to it of joy and sorrow, honor, shame and disgrace, as a mountain of lead stands before a little breath of wind."[26] Like the mountain, we remain rooted and unaffected by the passing mental phenomena. We let go by maintaining a receptive, free, open, clear field of consciousness that does not grab hold of any perceptible material as it passes through the still, silent, and interior nothingness.

To let go, one does not cling to passing mental phenomena like concepts, opinions, judgments, self-reflections, emotions, memories, and desires. To let go, one does not avoid or fight against incoming mental phenomena. To let go, one does not overreact, or react at all, to any mental content floating along the stream of consciousness. To let go, one does not interfere with or get involved with passing thoughts. In this state of mind, we discover our oneness with God, which can bubble up from within once we can see past all the mental junk.

By paying attention to God through a pure intention, the is-ness of the now, and interior nothingness we are, in fact, letting go of our attachment to thinking. Without engaging our self-talk, the soul silently rests in God within. Essentially, we are talking about meditation, or, as Eckhart describes it: "The central silence is there, where no creature may enter, nor any idea, and there the soul neither thinks nor acts, nor entertains any idea,

---

24. Harrington, *Dangerous Mystic*, 9.

25. Eckhart, *Meister Eckhart: Selected Writings*, 8.

26. Eckhart, *Meister Eckhart: The Essential Sermons*, 288.

either of itself or of anything else."[27] Detachment, living in God, cannot happen in our everyday lives without some form of meditation. Meister Eckhart would see a contemplative practice as essential to spiritual living. He would certainly recommend current contemplative prayer practices like Centering Prayer or Christian Meditation as ways of detaching and accessing the one ground of God and the soul.

We detach when we sit down to practice Centering Prayer or Christian meditation. Detachment as a contemplative practice builds on the two times a day we sit down to pray contemplatively. Detachment, for Eckhart, stretches into a continuous practice of contemplative prayer throughout the day. Eckhart connects contemplative prayer and daily life in this way: "Yet it is all one; for what we plant in the soil of contemplation we shall reap in the harvest of action, and thus the purpose of contemplation is achieved. There is a transition from one to the other but it is a single process with one end in view."[28] To practice detachment is to sink into nothing but God all day long. In this sense, it is contemplative living. Thomas Keating reflects, "Being in the presence of God as much as we can all day long is the secret of continuous growth in contemplative prayer."[29] Eckhart would agree.

THE BREAKTHROUGH

We live with a lot of protection. We each have a castle, moat, and round-the-clock guards checking every perimeter of the self. We can't do detachment on our own. Detachment finds its culmination in what Meister Eckhart calls the breakthrough. We need God. One of our biggest defenses is self-sufficiency, thinking we *can* do it on our own. By the breakthrough God shatters all these defenses, which keep reality out of our lives and, therefore, God, too.

Even when we commit to practicing detachment, it is not enough. We need God to do it: "this annihilation and diminution of self, however great a work it may be, will remain uncompleted unless it is God who completes it in the self."[30] God's completion of our detachment is what Eckhart calls the breakthrough. This is another of Eckhart's mystical themes. God needs to help us here because the ego will never let itself go. The ego can and will

27. Eckhart, *Meister Eckhart: A Modern Translation*, 96.

28. Eckhart, *Meister Eckhart: A Modern Translation*, 111.

29. Keating, *Fruits and Gifts of the Spirit*, 64.

30. Eckhart, *Meister Eckhart: The Essential Sermons*, 280.

turn the practice of detachment into yet another attachment. Moreover, there are things we just don't want to let go of. If the ego had a choice, it would always choose to cling to something. God has to help us here. God, in fact, initiates the practice of detachment and sustains us as we detach. Then, God finishes the job.

This truth about only God being able to detach us was brought home to me one day when my iPhone wouldn't turn on. I picked up my iPhone, assuming it was charged. When I turned it on, however, the screen remained blank. It would not turn on. My mind got swept up in a fury about the situation. Then, my iPhone powered on. Relieved, I realized how upset I had become. I reflected how I cannot detach all by myself. I need God to help me detach, to break through all attachments, the ego, and my illusory separation from God.

In one of his most well-known sermons, Eckhart contends that:

> In the breaking-through, when I come to be free of will of myself and of God's will and of all his works and of God himself, then I am above all created things, and I am neither God nor creature, but I am what I was and what I shall remain, now and eternally . . . in this breakthrough I receive that God and I are one.[31]

The breakthrough symbolizes that point at which God brings us into the ground and beyond all attachments. This is, as we have noted, something we cannot do on our own. God does it. God breaks through. Through God's grace we transcend all images, attachments, and distinction. Then, we enter fully into the one ground. The breakthrough represents the fullness and perfection of detachment. Breakthrough is the fulfillment of detachment in that all attachments are shed and we can enter the ground at long last.

In the breakthrough, we realize identical oneness with the Godhead. The soul breaks through to the ground where God's ground and the soul's ground are one, indistinct, and identical ground. We break through the Trinity into the Godhead of pure nothingness. Perfect detachment includes letting go of God. Eckhart famously prays in Sermon 52, "let us pray to God that we may be free of 'God.'"[32] The human person's breakthrough into the God beyond God takes the soul beyond the God whom we imagine is separate from us.

31. Eckhart, *Meister Eckhart: The Essential Sermons*, 203.
32. Eckhart, *Meister Eckhart: The Essential Sermons*, 200.

The breakthrough is more than a serene discovery of our true nature, though. It is a breaking down of cherished assumptions and a being broken through by the Godhead. There is a destruction of the shell, the separation, covering over oneness with God. Keel calls it "a radicalization of detachment."[33] It is radical because through the breakthrough, God attacks the root of our problem: thinking we are separate from God. God destroys this illusion and brings us into the ground. It is God erasing our illusions about being disconnected from all things. God breaks through all the walls our egoic minds have erected, which keep us from knowing our inherent oneness with the divine nothingness.

The transcendent nothingness helps us to let go of the separate God as well as the cherished beliefs that go along with it. Eckhart often tells us we must leave God behind. The breakthrough is a letting go of God. One of the last attachments to go is our ideas of God. Detachment and breaking through are an annihilation of all the things preventing us from enjoying oneness with God in the ground.

THE TRIAL OF MEISTER ECKHART

In 1327 Meister Eckhart traveled to Avignon to defend himself against accusations that his message was heretical. The accusations came from the archbishop of Cologne, Henry II of Virneburg. It seems likely this heresy hunting archbishop thought Meister Eckhart to be dangerous because his message became popular among the people. Before leaving for Avignon, in the Dominican church in Cologne, one of Eckhart's assistants publicly read a document Eckhart wrote affirming his innocence and willingness to renounce any errors the inquisitors found. By doing this, Eckhart undercut any charges of heresy. Henceforth, he could only be tried for spreading erroneous teaching. At the papal court he offered his defense, yet in 1329 Pope John XXII issued the papal bull "In the Field of the Lord." This bull condemned certain statements of the Meister's, but they were articles taken out of their original context.

Throughout his Inquisition, Eckhart practiced what he preached. During the trial he was perfectly willing to give up his life's work and submit to Church authority. He was not attached to his own spirituality. He did not have a tight mental grip on any of his ideas or concepts. He was quite open to admitting his errors and to renouncing them considering the Church's

33. Keel, *Meister Eckhart: An Asian Perspective*, 195.

authority to judge orthodoxy. I think this is a great testament to Eckhart's detachment. As a scholastic theologian and a preacher, words mattered to him. It is all too easy for such a person to identify with these roles and wind up a hypocrite. We have far too many examples today of people who proclaim their spiritual maturity but in truth lack it. Still, Eckhart shows he is not identified with his own spirituality and mystical system when he submits to Church authority. Truly, he had let go of himself.

Meister Eckhart says, "No one is happier than [the one] who has attained the greatest detachment."[34] By practicing detachment, we realize who we truly are and discover the truth of every other creature in the universe. We find God in all things. Eckhart offers this counsel:

> Detachment is the best of all, for it purifies the soul and cleanses the conscience and enkindles the heart and awakens the spirit and stimulates our longings and shows us where God is and separates us from created things and unites itself with God.[35]

In some unfathomable way, the world appears as it truly is: everything is sacred. The street, the bar, the nursery, the kitchen, the bedroom are all as holy as the tabernacle. Our call, according to Eckhart, is to drop the dividing line between sacred and secular. God is with us as we shop just as much as when we go to church. We must allow our whole lives to be prayer, and not rope off our prayer time from the rest of life. Yet, a concrete practice of meditation becomes more important than ever. Sinking down into God will never be constant unless we commit to a regular discipline of meditation. Eckhart stresses that we are to sink into the one ground at both specific times and all the time. This is how we practice detachment. We can then let go into God both in prayer and throughout our day. With this explosive awakening, we give birth to the realization that there is nothing but God.

REFLECTION QUESTIONS

1. What preoccupies you most of your day?
2. How can you practice detachment today?
3. What experiences suggest you need God to break through your attachments?

34. Eckhart, *Meister Eckhart: The Essential Sermons*, 293.
35. Eckhart, *Meister Eckhart: The Essential Sermons*, 294.

3

God Becomes Real

THE THIRD THEME INFORMING Meister Eckhart's mysticism is *the birth of the Word in the soul*. The Meister uses the birth to connect the Trinity, God becoming human in Jesus (or, incarnation), and our spiritual awakening. For Eckhart, the birth of the Word in the soul (our awakening) is one and the same as God the Father giving birth to the Son (in the Trinity) and the Son being born in time as Jesus of Nazareth (incarnation). All this will become clear as we delve into this mystical symbol of the birth.

Regarding our spiritual awakening, the symbol of birthing means *realizing God*. It is that moment of interior transformation when God becomes absolutely real to us. By the image of birthing, Eckhart describes how we wake up to the reality of God. But what does a spiritually awake person look like? The symbol of the birth addresses this question. Eckhart is clear that oneness with God looks like Jesus, or, more specifically, the inner state of our unity with God is the inner state of Jesus. As God becomes real to us, God births the Christ Mind in us (see Philippians 2:5). Then, we live with divine freedom or a life without why, which is another theme informing Meister Eckhart's mysticism. The only problem is that God is not real to most people.

WHEN GOD IS NOT REAL

Despite the faith-based roots of the United States, American society is already very secular, and growing more secular by the day. The category of "nones" is on the rise, which is the growing number of people in the United States who do not identify with any major religion. For many people today, God is not real. Why? Why is it the case that so many people find it hard to believe in God? Why do so many people feel like God is not real? For Eckhart, nothing is more real than God. The divine is Absolute Reality, in fact. Why isn't God real *for us*, though? Why isn't God real to our secular society, or even to many people in the pews?

Perhaps one major reason why God isn't real for us is our attachment to a rational and technological way of knowing. Our default assumptions are based on materialism, which is the belief that only physical matter exists. Our culture tends to put its faith only in what can be proved. We think only the physical is real, but not what goes on in our heads or our hearts. There is little room for mystery, unknowing, or uncertainty. If one cannot see it, touch it, or scientifically prove it, then we assume it isn't real. Many theologians sharply criticize this view as putting too much faith in science. Theologians like John Haught contend there is no experiment that can prove *only* the scientific method gives us access to truth. Of course, the scientific method provides truth. Haught is not criticizing the scientific method itself, but a kind of uncritical faith in science alone.[1] It's scientific, instead of religious, fundamentalism.

Furthermore, one does not have to be religious to find meaning. There are other options, such as atheism, agnosticism, and other indifferent attitudes to God. There are so many more niche hobbies and lifestyles than ever before that one can find enough meaning and a sense of community through a group formed around movies, skateboarding, fashion, philosophy, literature, or *Star Wars*. Religion and belief in God can be easily eclipsed in world filled with other options, even when these options have no reference to the transcendent.

Unfortunately, most of us don't know what we're missing. When God is not real to us, it's like we're drunk. Our perception is dulled. Our memory is foggy. At times, we even black out. Other times, everyday tasks seem dreamy. In short, the world of a drunk is a world of fantasy, seeing only what he wants to see or thinks he sees. Even worse, alcohol causes numerous bad life decisions and often results in a serious physical illness. When God isn't real to us our consciousness narrows and becomes dull, like that of a drunk. We lose spiritual health and things that would normally be treated as trivial get distorted into grave concerns. When God isn't real to

---

1. Haught, *God and the New Atheism*, 45.

us we wind up living in a fantasy world, the world of the ego. Such a world runs on ridiculous expectations, unexamined assumptions, attachments to things we desperately crave for happiness, and everything gets filtered through the attitude of how it is going to benefit *me*.

OUR UNKNOWN WINE CELLAR

There is a wonderful image for this situation that the Meister uses. In Sermon Ten Eckhart preaches:

> A person who is not at home with inward things does not know what God is. It is just like a man who has wine in his cellar and, having neither drunk nor even tried it, does not know that it is good. This is exactly the situation of people who live in ignorance: They do not know what God is and they think and fancy they are really living.[2]

Thus, Eckhart likens someone who does not know the God within to a person who has a basement full of choice wines but has never tried any. He doesn't know how good his wine is. Living ignorant of God is not living at all. Such people don't know how good they have it. They don't realize they are already one with God, and ultimate bliss is closer than they would believe.

Is this not our usual situation? We don't know how good our lives already are. Instead, we are always finding some reason to be unhappy. We are always comparing ourselves to others we find more successful, together, happy, or beautiful. If only I were like this or that celebrity! Then, I would surely be happy. Eckhart would say such people are living in ignorance because they do not know the transcendent gladness that is infinitely accessible within. The way we can access this transcendent gladness is go within ourselves, let go of our ideas of happiness, and let God be God. Detachment is required. Since our problem is ignorance, we live as if God were absent; we succumb to the illusion of being separate. This, however, is just a thought to let go of. Thomas Keating writes that:

> The chief thing that separates us from God is the thought that we are separated from God. If we get rid of that thought, our troubles will be greatly reduced. We fail to believe that we are always with God and that God is part of every reality. The present moment,

2. Eckhart, *Meister Eckhart: Teacher and Preacher*, 262.

every object we see, our inmost nature are all rooted in God. But we hesitate to believe this until personal experience gives us confidence to believe in it . . . The interior experience of God's presence activates our capacity to perceive God in everything else—in people, in events, in nature.[3]

By letting this thought of separation go and entering the ground we recognize what is already true: divine oneness. Once we truly see our oneness with God, we emerge from the darkness of spiritual ignorance into the light of awareness. That which is hidden within us comes to awareness. God is unveiled as the true ground upon which we have always been standing. This is the birth.

THE IMAGE OF BIRTHING

Watching my wife give birth to our two daughters is burned in my brain. While my wife was pregnant, we spent months preparing by getting all the necessary baby-related things and making a space in our home. Oddly, even though each time we were hyperaware that a little baby was coming into our lives, it wasn't quite real for us. That changed the moment each of my daughters was born. It became staggeringly real then! Once they were born, we recognized there was a life we had to care for. At the exact moment they were born, we knew only partially, minutely even, the enormous responsibility that comes with having a child. That reality only set in months, even years, later.

Besides the phase of getting ready, there was the actual birth. The experience of giving birth to each girl was different, that much was obvious even to me! My wife, Jessica, was in labor for over twenty-four hours with my first daughter. She told me how it felt like a marathon and there were times she thought her heart might give out because it was so exhausting, not to mention painful. Our second daughter was two weeks late and was induced. The whole thing was over in about seven minutes. Jessica seemed not to feel much at all. Giving birth is a messy and uncertain affair. Still, there is a point at which each baby girl became unflinchingly real for us. Such is the birth Eckhart is talking about.

The birth is God-realization; it is when God becomes clear, real, true, and present to us. God is and was always real, but we don't know it, experience it, or enjoy it. We are not aware. Hence, this realization is also called

3. Keating, *Open Mind, Open Heart*, 33–34.

an awakening. For the Meister this birth is the purpose of religion. As he preaches in Sermon 38:

> Why do we pray, why do we fast, why do we all perform our devotions and good works, why are we baptized, why did God, the All-Highest, take on our flesh?...in order that God may be born in the soul and the soul be born in God. That is why the whole of Scripture was written and why God created the whole world.[4]

For the Meister, there is no point to religion, to taking the spiritual journey, unless we are born in God and God is born in us. Birth symbolizes the integration of identity with God into life as a person distinct from God. As Michael Demkovich, a modern-day Dominican friar, expresses it: "Birthing allows something that is within to come to life . . . [God-birthing] allows the reality of God that is already in us to come to life in us."[5] Birthing, then, functions as a symbol of transformation.

Additionally, the birth symbolizes divine revelation, the revelation of God in us through the Son and the revelation of our inherent nature as the Son of God, the Christ. Birth serves as a symbol of the unveiling of our God-given Christ-nature. It is the bringing forth of what is within us— identity with God in the ground—into everyday life. The birth reveals our ground nature, *who we really are*. Eckhart says that through the birth, God both reveals the divine self and unveils our divine nature.

Eckhart stretches the metaphor of the birth in Sermon Six. As he preaches, he transcends each description to offer a more nondual vision. He starts with the Trinity. In giving birth to the Son, the Father and the Son are distinct while being the same. Then, Eckhart begins to go beyond traditional belief. Thus, he says, "Yet I say more: He has given birth to him in my soul."[6] The eternal birth beyond all existence happens in my soul. This birthing theme suggests distinction because someone gives birth to someone else: God the Father to the Son, and then God the Father to the soul. But, Eckhart keeps collapsing the distinctions between Father, Son, soul until there is *a Single One*, which is an alternate term he uses for the oneness of God and soul.

Eckhart continues, "He gives birth not only to me, his Son, but he gives birth to me as himself and himself as me and to me as his being and

---

4. Eckhart, *The Complete Mystical Works of Meister Eckhart*, 177.

5. Demkovich, *Introducing Meister Eckhart*, 98.

6. Eckhart, *Meister Eckhart: The Essential Sermons*, 187.

nature."[7] The birth is the ever-deepening and ongoing transformation of self-consciousness into divine consciousness, to which we are invited to consent continuously. Even more, it is the ultimate realization of our inherent identity with the God beyond God. If we let the birth happen as effortlessly as a mother lets a child grow within her, then gradually, imperceptibly and without our being aware, our divine self comes alive from within. Our I am is replaced by God's *I Am*. Our essence is revealed as the "being and nature" of God.

The birth, then, is our transformation into God. To illustrate this truth of the birth, Eckhart brings forth a central Christian mystery: the Eucharist. Just as many pieces of bread become One Body of Christ, many people realize the same divine oneness. Even more, Eckhart uses the Eucharist as a symbol of unity *and* distinction. There are many distinct pieces of bread yet One Body. Just so, I am distinct from the divine, but identical, too. Eckhart says we are so drastically transformed into God that we are utterly one. God gives us God in the birth so we may live the very life of the holy mystery. When we are changed into God, we realize our intrinsic divine oneness. *When we give birth to God we see there is nothing but God.*

THE NATURE OF A SPIRITUAL AWAKENING

We go through life asleep. The birth is our great awakening to *Reality As It Is*. Alas, most of us are still sleeping. In other words, we're living a rather unconscious life. Most of what we do, what we think, and what we feel is automatic. All we have to do is consider how a family member knows exactly what buttons to push to make us angry. There's this conditioning in us that disposes us to see reality in a very limited, narrow, and self-interested kind of way. That family member who can say just the right thing to make me angry is able to do so because I am so attached to or insecure about the thing being attacked. We go through life with this conditioning like walking around with an open gash in our bodies, draining our life force from us. Less graphically, our minds are so preoccupied with our psychological experience that we miss out on *Reality As It Is*. A story from the spiritual teacher and storyteller Anthony De Mello might help.

> A drunkard was walking down a street with blisters in both of his ears. A friend asked him what happened to cause the blisters.

7. Eckhart, *Meister Eckhart: The Essential Sermons*, 187.

"My wife left her hot iron on, so when the phone rang I picked up the iron by mistake." "Yes, but what about the other ear?" "The damned fool called back!"[8]

When we are asleep, many things can preoccupy our souls and arrest their spiritual development. For one, like the drunkard in the above story, we can keep repeating the same negative behavior, even when we know it hurts us.

We wake up from such unconsciousness when we give birth to the Word in our souls. Meister Eckhart says one major sign of the birth is the following, "what formerly was a hindrance for you is now a benefit to you. Your countenance will be completely turned toward this birth . . . Indeed, all things become for you nothing but God, for in all things you have your eye only on God."[9] Awakened by God, the things that tripped us up now serve as special conduits for practicing detachment and seeing God. And then, the way and the goal are one. If we have our eye, our awareness, trained to see God, we will see God everywhere. We will wake up. We see truly only when we practice seeing truly. We wake up by being aware. As Martin Laird says in *Into the Silent Land*:

> In order for awareness to drop its many scarves of self-conscious-ness and reveal its core—that overflowing vastness whose ground is God—we must firsts grow still. This is precisely where we meet the struggle of the human condition: we cannot be still. Even if the body can be still, the mind keeps racing like a runaway train. Our bodies may be at the place of prayer, but our minds are usu-ally not where our bodies are, but instead are at a shopping mall; on a beach in Majorca; reliving an argument; fearing the future; regretting the past; any place but right here in the simplicity of the present moment.[10]

The transformation that takes place in the birth of the Word within us is a something like a mind switch. Our consciousness switches to Christ Con-sciousness. The birth occurs when we live like Jesus, and we know it has happened when we are like Jesus. Eckhart closes a loop: we truly follow Jesus when we act like him by being totally fixed on God alone. In other words, oneness with God looks like Jesus on the cross who was completely surrendered to God in love and wholly centered on nothing but God. The oneness in Christ is the oneness in us. In Sermon 24, Eckhart says, "It is

8. De Mello, *Taking Flight*, 49.

9. Fox, *Passion for Creation*, 243.

10. Laird, *Into the Silent Land*, 49.

one, whatever it is in Christ, that it also is in you."[11] All that is required is to leave the self. We need to practice detachment by letting go, being aware, and centering our hearts on God alone like Jesus.

In Sermon One, Eckhart prays that God may help us to let Jesus into our souls so he can throw out everything that impedes being as one with God as he, Jesus, is. Eckhart asks where Jesus dwells in Sermon 58, and the answer is oneness with God the Father. Eckhart claims that is where we dwell, too. When we wake up, Eckhart says we "have grown into our Lord Jesus Christ inwardly and in all things so that all his works are reflected in us together with his divine image."[12] Thus, the spiritually awake person has the mind, the interior state, of Jesus Christ. This is the state in which God is real for us. To realize God is to realize I am one with God, for it is God's nature to be indistinct or one with everything.

The birth is awareness or spiritual sight. Eckhart describes it with the image of a barrel full of pure water. If we let the water become completely still, we can look into the water in the barrel and see our faces reflected back to us. This occurs when the water is still. All who are awake see the divine image reflected back to them in everything, and it happens when they are still inside, hence the need for a contemplative practice like Centering Prayer. When we are awake we see *reality just as it is* and not as we would like it to be. In that moment of pure seeing, we change.

HOW WE WAKE UP

How do we get here? How does God become real for us? How do we wake up? For Meister Eckhart it always comes down to detachment. That is the way, and we have already discussed it in the previous chapter. We will be delving further into detachment in the next chapter when we look at Meister Eckhart on nothingness.

Even though Eckhart's idea of detachment is rather straightforward, there are nuances to it. One of those nuances is love. The Meister sees detached love as central to the path of awakening to God's reality. The Meister does not separate love and detachment. Here are his thoughts on love from Sermon 27:

---

11. Eckhart, *Meister Eckhart: Teacher and Preacher*, 286.
12. Eckhart, *Meister Eckhart: Selected Writings*, 32.

Love is quite pure, quite bare, quite detached in itself. The greatest masters say that the love with which we love is the Holy Spirit . . . Love at its purest and most detached is nothing but God . . . Just as my eye cannot speak and my tongue cannot recognize colors, so love cannot incline to anything but goodness and God.[13]

Eckhart has a unique understanding of love. For him, to love is to detach from all those things that keep us locked away in a world of selfishness. When we love we are moved by the Holy Spirit so that our love is nothing but divine love. The most detached love is nothing but God. Love, then, is another way of putting the whole theme of this book and what I contend to be Eckhart's main message. Whenever we love, we grow closer to God. Loving makes us more like God. Loving not only unites us with God but also helps us realize *there is nothing but God* and that our truest and deepest self is divine.

Detached love is a significantly powerful path to the divine birth. Eckhart says our love has to be so unadorned and detached that it does not incline toward self, a special friend, or any one person *over* another. Detached love cares only for the other, and specifically the other *in God*. Further, this detached love is equal love. Eckhart calls on us to love all people equally, respecting and regarding all people in an equal manner. He doesn't want us to make any distinctions between people, because in the one ground there are no distinctions. Every single person is one in the ground.

When speaking of love, Eckhart likes to quote St. Augustine who says whatever we love we become. Eckhart then comments, "In the love that a man gives there is no duality but one and unity, and in love I am God more than I am in myself . . . man can become God in love."[14] Love is nondual and one, indistinct from God. Loving is, then, a major way we realize our indistinct unity with God. Love is how we wake up to God's reality in our lives and as our deepest self. Just to love is the path and it is the core of the Gospel, as Jesus himself teaches, "Love one another as I have loved you" (John 13:34).

GOD'S JOY IN THE BIRTH

The birth is a joyful experience. It is a joy for us because we come to know the eternal source of happiness, God. But, it is also a joy for God. Like a

13. Eckhart, *The Complete Mystical Works of Meister Eckhart*, 99.

14. Eckhart, *The Complete Mystical Works of Meister Eckhart*, 105.

good parent, God rejoices over us throughout our lives, whether we are spiritually awake or not. For those of us who are parents, there is a sort of unconditional joy over our children. We are happy with them at some foundational level no matter what they do, simply rejoicing over their simple existence not because of anything they do. Even when they scream awake at two, three, and four in the morning, they are our joy. Even when they take a box of cereal and shake it so violently that the cereal flies out all over the kitchen, we take tremendous delight in our kids. Just so, God takes tremendous delight in us, and enjoys our birth.

God gives the divine nature in the birth so that we can enjoy it. Now, when we enjoy God divinely, we know this heavenly sufficiency. Enjoying the divine nature as God does means on God's terms, as Thomas Keating would say. We enjoy God on God's terms when we enjoy God as mystery, in silence and non-thinking nothingness. Once we love, let go, and become silent within through a contemplative practice like Centering Prayer or the Jesus Prayer, God is born. Then, everything we do is divine. Then, God is real for us and divine joy pours into the world through us.

Eckhart poetically describes the birth as God giving God and taking pleasure in such giving in Sermon 59:

> God takes all his pleasure in this birth, and he gives birth to his Son in us so that we have all our pleasure in it and so that we give birth to this same natural Son together with him. For God has all his pleasure in this birth and for this reason he gives birth to himself in us, so that he might have all his pleasure in the soul and that we might have all our pleasure in him.[15]

The birth of the Word in our souls is God's absolute pleasure! God explodes with unfathomable joy in the birth, when God reveals, gives, and awakens us to the divine life. Indeed, all God's joy is found in the unity we have and realize through the birth.

Eckhart uses a wonderful image to communicate the joy God has in our unity or, to use his word, sameness:

> Now all things are alike in God and are God himself. Here in this sameness God finds it so pleasant that he lets his nature and his being flow in this sameness in himself. It is just as enjoyable for him as when someone lets a horse run loose on a meadow that is completely level and smooth. Such is the horse's nature that it pours itself out with all its might in jumping about the meadow.

15. Eckhart, *Meister Eckhart: Teacher and Preacher*, 308.

> This it would find delightful; such is its nature. So, too, does God
> find delight and satisfaction where he finds sameness. He finds it a
> joy to pour his nature and his being completely into the sameness,
> for he is this sameness himself.[16]

Just as a horse takes delight in what it is, we take delight in who we are, and God takes delight in who God is. This delight is all one and the same because all things are one with God in the ground. There, in this sameness, nothing can disturb us or grieve us. For, by the birth we can never lose God. Playing with this image of the birth, Eckhart says, "All that I have by birth can be taken from me by no one."[17] We cannot lose God. God cannot be taken away from us, for we always already have God within us. We have God as our birthright. God doesn't want us to lose God: "This is why God gives birth to himself into me fully, so that I may never lose him."[18] This stabilizes us and frees us from anxiety. It allows us to live with real freedom.

A SPONTANEOUS LIFE—LIVING WITHOUT WHY

Life after the birth bears fruit in a major way: our motives get clarified. Before the birth we might be like the adults in the following story from Anthony De Mello.

> Three grown-ups were having morning coffee in the kitchen while
> the children played on the floor. The conversation turned on what
> they would do if danger threatened and each of the grown-ups
> said that the first thing they would do was save the children. Sud-
> denly the safety valve of the pressure cooker burst, creating an
> explosion of steam in the room. Within seconds everyone was out
> of the kitchen—except for the kids playing on the floor.[19]

The grown-ups in this story think they would act generously and heroically. But, they each have a hidden agenda. After the birth, we live without a hidden agenda. Even though these grown-ups said they'd look out for the children's safety first, their real agenda was to look out for themselves. Eckhart would say these parents have a "why."

16. Eckhart, *Meister Eckhart: Teacher and Preacher*, 269.

17. Eckhart, *Meister Eckhart: Teacher and Preacher*, 308.

18. Eckhart, *Meister Eckhart: Teacher and Preacher*, 308.

19. De Mello, *Taking Flight*, 148.

The fifth theme in Meister Eckhart's mysticism is *living without a why*. This phrase communicates a purposeless activity and existence. It describes a life that is gratuitous, fully in the moment, enjoying the activity of the now, and not harboring expectations or anxious goals about the future. It springs from the birth. "And so the Son is born in us in that we are without a why and are born again into the Son."[20] This is the kind of life that lives life simply for itself and for no ulterior motive. Living without why means not looking for results or treating something as a means to an end. Everything is its own end and is enjoyed on its own terms. Mow the lawn to mow the lawn. Wash the dishes to wash the dishes. Write just to write. Yes, there may be reasons we do these things, but they are not primary reasons or the real motivation. Living without why truly symbolizes a life that simply enjoys God in the moment, whatever that moment may be.

The texture of all our activity once we live from the one ground is the spontaneous freedom of nondual love. When we are one with God, we love as God loves, and that is in a spontaneously free and joyful way. Eckhart's living without a why is about disinterested love. Sermon 28 says, "whoever dwells in the goodness of his nature, dwells in God's love: but love is without Why."[21] Divine love loves simply to love, not for any particular reason. In other words, with his term "living without a why" Eckhart is emphasizing the utter gratuitousness of love. Divine gratuitousness, then, expresses the life lived from the ground.

What does it mean to live without a why? Eckhart teases out a meaning by comparing our efforts at good works to a bad gardener in Sermon 39. He says we act like a gardener whose job is to plant a beautiful garden but instead uproots all the existing trees. We work for reasons other than God and expect to get something from our efforts. Just so, the gardener in Eckhart's little parable ruins the garden before he even begins planting and expects to be paid for it.[22] Doing things on our own, under our own steam, is to do it with ego, separated from God. Such works only encourage more division. Such works only sever relationships between people, the rest of creation, and God. Doing work with a why (ego agenda) uproots those works from the one ground. Instead of letting all works be grounded in God, the ego digs them up out of the one ground and, thus, disconnects them from the dynamic soil of God's love.

---

20. McGinn, *The Mystical Thought of Meister Eckhart*, 154.

21. Eckhart, *The Complete Mystical Works of Meister Eckhart*, 129.

22. Eckhart, *Meister Eckhart: Teacher and Preacher*, 296.

When we are living without a why, God hurries to transform us. God wants to bring the Son to birth in us and to birth us into the Godhead, which makes us realize we are one with the holy mystery in the one ground. In other words, it is God living in, through, with, and *as* self and self living *as* God. It is living life inside-out. Being grounded in God within enables us to engage all of creation with freedom, compassion, and justice. The Meister preaches in Sermon 39:

> In the just nothing should work but God alone. If it happens that anything from without moves you to work, the works are really all dead. And if it happens that God moves you from without to work, these works are all dead. If your works are to live, God must move you from within, in the innermost of the soul, if they really are to live.[23]

Eckhart contends that compulsive work deadens the soul. Having an outside thing move us to action betrays a certain enslavement. We get attached to following rules and reacting to life from the ego. Often, we are compelled to do something. This compulsion comes from outside. It comes from a boss, circumstances, rules, etc. Instead, Eckhart counsels us to work from our inner core, from within. The energy to do must come from within us, from where we are most truly ourselves: the one ground.

We react negatively when we're forced to do something while at other times we're not interested in what we're doing because it's only a means to an end, to getting the thing we really want. Eckhart sees a disconnect here. He sees from the perspective of the ground, where all things are one. When we are compelled to work, for results, Eckhart sees such work reinforcing the illusion that everything is split. The interior, why we work, is not aligned with the exterior, that is, with the work we do. Thus, Eckhart solves the issue by inviting us to let God move us from within, from the ground. We need to enter our own ground, which is God's ground, and work from there. The point is to act with contemplative silence and interior nothingness in daily life. Such work lacks any why.

FORREST GUMP

The movie *Forrest Gump*, starring Tom Hanks as Forrest Gump, portrays a man who lives without why. Forrest never has an ulterior motive. He is

---

23. Eckhart, *Meister Eckhart: Teacher and Preacher*, 297.

pure. He acts entirely out of love, often despite what people think of him. He appears to fully accept whatever happens based on a piece of wisdom he learned from his mother: "Life is like a box of chocolates. You never know what you're gonna get." He acts selflessly when he rushes into the jungles of Vietnam to save his friend Bubba, and he ends up saving several other men. Even though his friend Bubba died, Forrest acted altruistically.

People around Forrest used him for their own purposes. His football coach called him a "stupid son of a bitch" but didn't care because he ran so fast he would win games for them. Forrest, though, didn't use people. He cared for them. He was a remarkably simple person, in the best sense of the word. Without an agenda, he was present in the moment. He was focused on the person in front of him. He could have been even wealthier after the success of his shrimping business, but he only went into it after his good friend, Bubba, asked him. After Bubba died, Forrest honored his memory by making good on his promise to join Bubba on a shrimp boat. This promise extended to Bubba's impoverished family. Again, to be faithful to his friend, Forrest gives half of the money made through shrimping to Bubba's family, who become instant millionaires!

A life without why and detached love come together in Forrest's devotion to Jenny, his childhood friend. As soon as he sees Jenny in trouble, he comes running to help her. For instance, he defends her honor when she's playing at a burlesque house and some guy harasses her. He proves his love for her as she constantly runs away with man after man by being there for her whenever her life falls apart. At one point, Jenny comes to live with Forrest, and he confesses his love for her. Jenny says he doesn't know what love is. But, again, being true and honest, Forrest replies that he does indeed know what love is, even though he isn't a smart man. Still, through it all, Forrest remains true to Jenny, especially when she dies and leaves him with a son he does not know. Forrest takes the boy into his home and raises him with utmost love. In college, Jenny asks Forrest if he ever dreams of who he is going to be. Forrest replies, "Who I'm gonna be? Aren't I going to be me?" He's so free of agenda that he knows who he is and doesn't need to be anyone else. This is the fruit of a life without why: knowing who you are.

A WELL-EXERCISED GROUND

Why-less action characterizes a life lived from the one ground of God and the soul. Eckhart says as much in Sermon Five-b, "God's ground is my ground and my ground is God's ground. Here I live on my own as God lives on his own. All our works should work out of this innermost ground without a why or a wherefore."[24] A spontaneous, faithful, and selfless life flows from our identity with God in the ground. The Meister provides an example of this grounded living by turning a well-known Gospel story on its head in Sermon 86. That story is the scene of Martha and Mary in the Gospel of Luke. Briefly put, Martha seems to be anxious that she is doing all the kitchen work while Mary is listening to Jesus teach. For most of Christian history, theologians and saints have praised Mary for choosing "the better part" and have seen this as a confirmation that contemplation is better than action.

Eckhart, though, praises Martha for being unimpeded by works, by activity, and being free down to her ground. Martha, he says, asked Jesus to tell Mary to get up from listening to him because she feared Mary might become attached to the consoling experience of being near Jesus. Hence, according to Eckhart, Jesus commends Martha. The one thing needed, Jesus tells Martha, is God and she has God. She lives and works from her own ground with freedom from all attachments. She stands in the middle of people, things, and events. Yet, they do not hinder her. This is how it should be for those of us who are awake and live without why.

So, work from your ground. Be grounded in God always, for we are often un-grounded, disconnected, alone, and adrift. Enter the one ground. Rest there. Let all you do proceed from the one ground, then all you do will be divine (even eating, walking, cleaning, smiling). Let all your actions be grounded in God. Open to the silent ground within during work. Let "your" work be divine; let "your" actions be the One welling up. Let the ground surface as you work.

A well-exercised ground, a life of why-less activity, is a just life. The issue of justice is a central concern for the Meister. No one can claim oneness with God unless they are living in justice. The one who is awake has been changed into justice. Such a person abides in the mystery of God to the extent of identifying with the divine nature. This is a just person, that is, one in whom God gives birth to the Word and who is born back into God. This means the just person gives flesh to God in the world and realizes divine identity. Eckhart says that realizing we are identical with God in the ground results in a new way of living in the world. The result is justice, which starts with a life lived from the one ground. According to Eckhart, the just person

24. Eckhart, *Meister Eckhart: The Essential Sermons*, 183.

has no hidden motives or selfish agenda in his works. The just person has no "why" in her or his works. The just person works for no reward, for no reason at all. Living without why makes us dangerous, because once God is the center, everything on the periphery is relativized. The things our culture assumes are important become unimportant. This makes the just person dangerous because she or he is not invested in the things of this the world.

One consequence of living without why and from a well-exercised ground is that we keep nothing from God. However, we like to compartmentalize. We like to organize things, keep them in proper order, and in a designated place. We file, label, box, and pile. We like keeping things separate. Have you ever seen a store called "The Container Store"? This place is full of containers: boxes, organizers, space-savers, drawers, and more. It seems that compartmentalizing is ingrained in us. This tendency, however, can affect our spiritual lives negatively. Our oneness with God is never set-off and separate from the rest of our life. The ground can't be filed away only to be pulled out at a time of our choosing; we cannot hermetically seal off the holy mystery from everyday existence. Keeping God in a compartment labeled "Sunday morning" prevents divine transformation—the birth—from happening. Eckhart advocates integrating our spirituality with our daily lives by always remaining in the ground and going about our day grounded in the ground that has no why or wherefore. This is what it means to live detachment.

LET THE BIRTH HAPPEN

All that is within God moves God to transform us by drawing us into the ground and giving birth to us as the Son. God's business is the business of transformation. There is a pressure coming from within God to share divinity with all, to enable all creation to discover its radical self-same identity with the divine nothing. In other words, the Father wants us to become Christ. God is consumed with the eternal birth, wanting it to happen to us, through us, and in us. All God's pleasure and delight consists in giving birth, in the Triune self-giving love, in loving us and in waking us up. The birth is divine gift as well as the divinity coming alive in us. We give birth to God, we wake up to the holy mystery within us, as we continuously let go and love in a detached way.

Your task is to let it happen. Do not be concerned with making it happen, that is God's arena. Your job is to detach from ego and let the mystery of the Godhead bring you into the ground. In the one ground, you will be born another Christ. Birthing the Word, you will realize just how real God is. You will wake up to the truth. You will then live without any hidden motive. You will lack any why.

The pressure moving God to give birth and transform us is nothing other than love. Eckhart goes so far as to say that the very essence of the Trinity lies in our transformation: "the Father's being consists in giving birth to the Son; the Son's being consists in my being born in him and like him; the Holy Spirit's being lies in my catching fire and becoming totally melted and becoming simply love."[25] God wants us to melt away into love. God wants us to receive so much divine love that all distinction becomes vaporized and only love remains. Simply put, we are love. God wants us to realize our true essence: selfless love.

Our true essence appears only when we detach. Then, our awareness changes. We experience a birth of spiritual awareness, which is a bringing forth into consciousness of the reality of God within us. Eckhart wants nothing less than a total revolution of our interior world. He wants to reorient it away from self and towards the God who is always and forever one with us. The birth is the transformative process whereby we realize we are one with God and integrate that truth into our daily lives. Eckhart preaches to bring us to this new, transformed awareness. It is, of course, nothing but awareness of what is always already true: God is, God is one, and God is beyond all. More cryptically, the birth is the awakening of the nothingness of God within.

REFLECTION QUESTIONS

1. Is God real for you? Why or why not?

2. When have you experienced a spiritual awakening? When have you realized you were not seeing *reality as it is*?

3. When do you do things for "outside" reasons?

4. Is your love for your family and friends a detached love? Why or why not?

25. Eckhart, *Meister Eckhart: Teacher and Preacher*, 298.

4

Nothingness

MEISTER ECKHART RARELY TALKS about his personal experience. There are only a handful of times, and often they are asides to his main point. However, Sermon 71 contains a passage that some scholars believe might be a direct report of his own mystical experience. The Meister says, "It seemed to a man as though in a dream—it was a waking dream—that he became pregnant with nothing as a woman does with child, and in this nothing God was born; he was the fruit of the nothing. God was born in the nothing."[1] Nothingness, then, figures prominently in his own experience of God. Also, nothingness has ties to all of his major themes: the ground, detachment, the breakthrough, the birth, and "whyless" action. Nothingness can be a synonym, at times, for the ground and for the path of detachment, for instance. Therefore, it is fair to describe Meister Eckhart's mysticism as a mysticism of nothingness.

When Meister Eckhart preaches nothingness, he intends to disrupt our pedestrian ways of conceiving God and ourselves. To be faithful to Eckhart, the present chapter may come across as subversive, radical, and purposefully shocking. Further, by the word "nothing," the Meister does not mean that God does not exist. Eckhart was a Dominican friar and a Catholic priest. The faith was his life. He once preached, "God is nothing: not in the sense of having no being. He is neither *this* nor *that* that one can speak of: He is being above all being. He is beingless being."[2] Therefore, if this chapter feels negative, please remember that Eckhart constantly stretches

1. Eckhart, *Meister Eckhart: Teacher and Preacher*, 323.
2. Eckhart, *The Complete Mystical Works of Meister Eckhart*, 316–17.

language to its breaking point in order to communicate the splendorous truth of the God revealed in Jesus Christ. Truly, the word "nothing" is not the final word about God or our relationship with God. Finally, as shown by Eckhart's own reported experience, nothingness is intrinsically linked to the birth of the Word in our souls along with the peace, freedom, bliss, and love that flow from realizing God in our lives.

Now, "nothing" is a loaded term for Meister Eckhart. He assigns the word four meanings in Sermon 71, which is a reflection on Acts 9:8: "Paul rose from the ground and with eyes open he saw nothing." Eckhart unfolds his interpretation of this line:

> One meaning is: When he got up from the ground, with eyes open he saw nothing, and the nothing was God; for when he saw God, he [Luke] calls this a nothing. The second: When he got up he saw nothing but God. The third: In all things he saw nothing but God. The fourth: When he saw God, he viewed all things as nothing.[3]

Using these four meanings, we will delve further into Meister Eckhart's mysticism of nothingness. First, the phrase "he saw nothing, and the nothing was God" raises the challenging idea that God is nothing. Second, the phrase "he saw nothing but God" takes us into a discussion of indistinct nothingness, or nonduality and nothingness. Third, the phrase "In all things he saw nothing but God" provides an opportunity to discuss the path of nothingness. Fourth, and finally, the phrase "When he saw God, he viewed all things as nothing" provides an opportunity to examine how to practice nothingness.

GOD IS NOTHING

Let's look at the first phrase from Sermon 71, "he saw nothing, and the nothing was God." According to Meister Eckhart, *God is nothing*. This statement is an example of the apophatic way, which is devoted to denying all our words for and thoughts of God. In this approach, we uncover the real God, not the God made up of our words, our thoughts, or our theologies. In effect, Eckhart is showing us how to respect God as mystery and what this means for our prayer lives. The apophatic way is the way of negation. It is the negation of God. As my old theology professor used to say, the apophatic way means saying, "That's not God. That's not God. That's not God."

---

3. Eckhart, *Meister Eckhart: Teacher and Preacher*, 320.

God is light. No, that's not God. God is truth. No, that's not God. God is a being. No, that's not God. God is life. No, that's not God. The divine reality is not any of these ideas or experiences simply because the divine reality transcends all of them.

The apophatic way is based on the first commandment, namely that we are to have no idols but worship God alone. The apophatic tradition builds on this fundamental commandment and Jesus' own teaching on non-idolatry: "No one can serve two masters. He will either hate one and love the other, or be devoted to one and despise the other. You cannot serve God and mammon" (Matt 6:24). One of the subtlest idols we can worship is our image or idea of God. Eckhart tells a story about this in Sermon 53: "We read of one good man who was entreating God in his prayer and wanted to give names to him. Then a brother said: 'Be quiet—you are dishonoring God.' We cannot find a single name we might give to God."[4] He also says, "God is nameless, because no one can say anything or understand anything about him." Because all language limits God, Eckhart reminds us that all knowing must be abandoned for the unknowing in which we really know God.

Meister Eckhart recognizes that our rational way of knowing cannot grasp the mystery of God. This qualifies his own sermons. Neither words nor thoughts grasp God. The divine reality is unimaginably strange to us. Not only does God transcend our minds, but also being itself. Thus, Eckhart often refers to God as "nothing." In Sermon 83, he calls God the "nothingness, for which there is no name."[5] Eckhart is not saying God does not exist. Rather, the divine nothing means God is above being. In Sermon Nine, Eckhart discusses how God transcends being:

> Whatever has being, time, or place does not touch God. He is above it . . . Unsophisticated teachers say that God is pure being. He is as high above being as the highest angel is above a gnat. I would be speaking as incorrectly in calling God a being as if I called the sun pale or black. God is neither this nor that.[6]

Divine nothingness radicalizes the absolute mystery of God and overturns all divine names. In fact, nothingness appears so often in Eckhart's mysticism, it connects the mystery of God, mystical identity with God, the soul, and detachment. Eckhart uses "nothingness" to describe all of them.

4. Eckhart, *Meister Eckhart: The Essential Sermons*, 204.
5. Eckhart, *Meister Eckhart: The Essential Sermons*, 207.
6. Eckhart, *Meister Eckhart: Teacher and Preacher*, 256.

MYSTICAL ATHEISM

Meister Eckhart's mysticism of nothingness holds, I believe, great promise for responding to the atheism of our time. Some scholars have labelled Meister Eckhart's mysticism a sort of "mystical atheism" because he threatens traditional belief in God. He attempts to free people from a limited and ultimately idolatrous understanding of God as a supreme being. Meister Eckhart peels back all our images and thoughts to help us peek at the divine nothingness beyond existence. Speaking of God in Sermon 23, Eckhart denies the classic names for God then asks, "But if God is neither goodness nor being nor truth nor one, what then is He? He is pure nothing; he is neither this nor that."[7] There is no God as we normally understand the word, "God."

In Sermon 83, the Meister wisely says our images for God say more about us than they do about God. We project our needs, wants, and wishes onto God. It seems Eckhart has anticipated the critique of religion leveled by some arch-atheists like Ludwig Feuerbach, Karl Marx, and Sigmund Freud! We often relate to a God of our own imagining. If we project our own conceptions of God based on ourselves, we can fall into the trap of trying to control God.

All too often the God we believe in and theologize about is an idol. We craft God in our own image to manipulate and use for our own purposes. The preacher who hates homosexuals uses a vengeful God to back up his perverse ideology. The religious terrorist glories in a wrathful God who intends to wipe out the infidels. The chaplain of the rich and powerful conveniently overlooks Jesus' teaching on renouncing possessions and caring for the poor in favor of a prosperity Gospel. Believers of all stripes and political persuasions bow to capitalism, even though Jesus clearly says one cannot worship God and money. As Eckhart scholar Charlotte Radler puts it, each one:

> is ultimately a projection of the human being's wishes, desires, and needs, and, thus, is an idol. The best way to honor 'God' is, thus, to dive into 'a-theism' and not to have a 'God,' that is, to let God be nothing and exist in the same nothingness . . . The Dominican Master, hence, fractures the hegemony of theism and embraces an 'atheism,' which unmasks the golden calf, which humans call 'God.'[8]

7. Eckhart, *The Complete Mystical Works of Meister Eckhart*, 287.
8. Radler, "Losing the Self," 112.

This projected God is but a human construct, a thing people have made much as the Israelites fashioned a golden calf to worship while Moses was on Mount Sinai. The major problem both the Israelites and contemporary peoples have is the tendency to treat God as a thing. Theologian David Bentley Hart articulates the precise sense in which atheism *and* religion often make this mistake:

> The most pervasive error one encounters in contemporary arguments about belief in God . . . is the habit of conceiving of God simply as some very large object or agency within the universe, or perhaps alongside the universe, a being among other beings, who differs from all other beings in magnitude, power, and duration, but not ontologically, and who is related to the world more or less as a craftsman is related to an artifact.[9]

For Eckhart, God is too real merely to exist. Things and people exist. The divine, however, is the very ground of existence. God exists, but beyond human conception and language. Even more, nothingness means divinity transcends time, space, and even being itself. Now, for Eckhart, this does not mean that we cannot access God. He is quite insistent, as we saw in previous chapters, that God is not only within us, but also one with us.

This divine as no-thing helps make sense of how we experience God. I believe Eckhart's nothingness responds to our culture's sense of divine absence. It seems that many of us—religious and non-religious alike—do not see that God is present in our lives. When we pray, we feel like the only answer we receive is silence. Here is common ground between believers and unbelievers: nothingness. When confronted with the contemporary complaints like "I feel distant from God," "I don't even know if there is a God," or "there's no evidence for God," Eckhart would likely respond by saying, "God is nothing, so let yourself be reduced to nothing and you will discover the truth."

The Meister preaches this mystical atheism in his famous Sermon 52 on the first beatitude, "Blessed are the poor in spirit" (Matthew 5:3). He says, "I pray God to free me of God, for my real being is above God if we take God to be the beginning of created things."[10] I am above God the creator because "in the same being of God where God is above being and above distinction, there I myself was."[11] He is talking about the ground,

9. Hart, *The Experience of God*, 32.
10. Eckhart, *Meister Eckhart: The Essential Sermons*, 202.
11. Eckhart, *Meister Eckhart: The Essential Sermons*, 202.

where the soul is identical with the God beyond God. Eckhart prays to become free of the God that is an object of consciousness in order to awaken to the God beyond God. Now, he also says, "God is neither being nor rational, and that he does not know this or that. Therefore God is free of all things, and therefore he is all things."[12] God is nothing and not *a* being. We must go beyond the duality of God and creature. For Meister Eckhart, our God is not "a god," but may be better understood as the *godless nothingness*. Since the divine reality is absolutely transcendent and beyond being, no name and no understanding will ever grasp the divine reality. Eckhart still believes in God, just not the God most of us grew up believing. He prods us to let go of "God" for the sake of God. This involves a surrender of all distinction between the divine and the soul as well as a severe detachment from the God of standard religion. Letting go of God for God is to let go, simultaneously, of the separate God and the separate self. It is to taste fully Eckhart's startlingly attractive statement: "The eye in which I see God is the same eye in which God sees me."[13] This is the godless nothing who is beyond all gods and still absolutely one with us.

INDISTINCT NOTHINGNESS:
OUR REAL IDENTITY

Now, the second phrase from Sermon 71 reads, "he saw nothing but God," where "he" refers to St. Paul. The core idea here is the core idea of this book, which is *nothing but God*. According to Eckhart, St. Paul saw nothing but the God who is nothing. Since God is nothing, God is also everything. There is nothing but the divine nothing. *Nothing but God* means indistinct nothingness.

Eckhart asserts that the divine is not something in particular. God is a lot like space. The seemingly endless emptiness of outer space provides a backdrop for planets, galaxies, and light to stand out. But space is not anything in particular. Just so, indistinction means God is not some-thing: "God and the soul are so entirely one that God cannot have a single distinctive feature separating Him from the soul and making Him different . . . He and the soul and so entirely one that God cannot have any quality such that we can say anything, or nothing, about God that points to difference or

12. Eckhart, *Meister Eckhart: The Essential Sermons*, 201.
13. Eckhart, *Meister Eckhart: Teacher and Preacher*, 270.

otherness."[14] Being indistinct allows God to be everything. In other words, God is our deepest identity because God is no particular thing. As James Finley, a former Trappist monk who studied under Thomas Merton, explains the indistinct nature of God:

> If God were something (some thing) he would not be ALL, for we would have but to find one grain of sand to find some thing he is not and thereby deprive him of being ALL. But since God is nothing (no thing) he moves in perfect freedom as the ground, the source, the fulfillment, the no-thing that sustains all things.[15]

To know this, for Eckhart, is to know truth. Paul is struck by the light, enlightened, to see this truth. All things are the divine nothing because there is nothing but God. Eckhart proclaims to us "the 'nothing' whose light is all lights, whose being is all beings."[16] Essentially, each of us is the divine nothing because the divine nothing is the being of all things.

God is both our deepest identity and radically, infinitely other than us. Since we are "made in God's image, we too are no-thing. As persons we shall find our fulfillment not in any thing but only in a total union and identification with God in love."[17] The depth of all things is the holy mystery, because everything has its reality in God and "whatever is in God, *is* God," as Eckhart says in Sermon Three.[18] The core reality of every creature is the divine nothing. Speaking of the apostle John in Sermon 61, Eckhart preaches, "he recognized nothing as God and everything as Godly."[19] There is nothing but the divine nothing.

However, our essence is often confused with our form. All too often, *who we really are* is mistaken for the *surface* of who we are. Anthony De Mello tells the story of an unnamed spiritual master who recognizes this truth of identity and nothingness:

> The Master claimed that it made no sense at all to define oneself as Indian, Chinese, African, American, Hindu, Christian, or Muslim, for these are merely labels. To a disciple who claimed he was Jewish first, last, and above all else, the Master said benignly, "Your conditioning is Jewish, not your identity." "What's my identity?"

---

14. Eckhart, *The Complete Mystical Works of Meister Eckhart*, 263.

15. Finley, *Merton's Palace of Nowhere*, 142.

16. Eckhart, *Meister Eckhart: Teacher and Preacher*, 324.

17. Finley, *Merton's Palace of Nowhere*, 142.

18. Eckhart, *Meister Eckhart: Teacher and Preacher*, 246.

19. Demkovich, *Introducing Meister Eckhart*, 61.

"Nothing," said the Master. "You mean I am an emptiness and a void?" asked the incredulous disciple. "Nothing that can be labeled," said the Master.[20]

Our identity is deeper than any label. Our truest and deepest identity, deeper than any nationality, ethnicity, religion, or way of life, is found in the divine nothing.

This mystical truth, "the nothing whose light is all lights, whose being is all beings," has profound and life-altering implications for each one of us.[21] A creature, in God, *is* the divine nothing. No form comprises our true essence. Rather, all things are the divine nothing, because there is nothing but God. Here, Eckhart uses the word "nothing" in a way similar to the word "ground." In Sermon Five-b Eckhart says, "God's ground is my ground, and my ground is God's ground."[22] He could use the same construction in Sermon 71, "God's nothingness is my nothingness, and my nothingness is God's nothingness."

The mind-blowing truth is that *the self is the divine nothing.* That's the core identity of the soul. As Charlotte Radler says, "the self's only true existence is the divine nothingness."[23] This is a truth we realize only through the letting go. The atmosphere of divine transformation is nothingness: "God was born in the nothing."[24] The way of divine transformation is nothingness: "When the soul comes into the One and there enters into a pure rejection of itself, it finds God as in a nothing."[25] The nothingness of God is the essence of all created things: "in God there is nothing but God. When I know all creatures in God, I know nothing."[26] The goal of transformation is the realization of identity with the divine nothing, which happens through detachment or dis-identifying with all my surface identities.

As the divine nothing, our real identity is sheer gift and not some-*thing* we make ourselves. We may be free to decide for ourselves, but we are not the ultimate masters of our fates. It is a healthy stability in a world of hyper fast change and, at times, chaos. As the globe gets smaller, science probes further, and cultures mingle, tightly held identities can fracture.

20. De Mello, *Awakening*, 74.

21. Eckhart, *Meister Eckhart: Teacher and Preacher*, 324.

22. Eckhart, *Meister Eckhart: The Essential Sermons*, 183.

23. Radler, "Losing the Self," 112.

24. Eckhart, *Meister Eckhart: Teacher and Preacher*, 323.

25. Eckhart, *Meister Eckhart: Teacher and Preacher*, 323.

26. Eckhart, *Meister Eckhart: Teacher and Preacher*, 323.

Our identity as the divine nothing provides a rock-solid security in an otherwise incredibly insecure world. This divine identity means our deepest self can never be hurt. Trauma, of course, is all-too-real. But our deepest self is invulnerable because it is the divine nothing, and hence, transcendent. Finally, since the self is the divine nothing, and the divine nothing is incomprehensible, our true essence is incomprehensible. There will never be an end to discovering more of God and more of ourselves. It is an endlessly fascinating mystery, luring us into its unfathomable depths of eternal delight. To me, this means that knowing that the one mystery of who I am and who God is will be eternally exciting!

Since the self is the divine nothing, we are only bound by the things that we let define us. There is no definition, no label, no physical aspect, no mental construct, no ethnicity, and no religion capable of defining our authentic identity. No one is chained to any of these self-concepts. This is our liberation. This is our enlightenment. God is born as we let go of false identities in the silence of prayer and in experiences of daily life. This is another dimension of what the birth means for Eckhart: the core of our selfhood as the divine nothing emerges into consciousness. The Meister, perhaps with some mischievous glee, paradoxically instructs us that "all our being consists in nothing but becoming nothing."[27] It is this nothing, this silence and solitude, that defines us. It is not, however, a negative experience. Thomas Keating writes that "interior silence or 'resting in God' is beyond thinking, images, and emotions. This awareness tells you that the core of your being is eternal and indestructible and that you as a person are loved by God and share his divine life."[28] Infinite love flows like a powerful spring from the discovery of this divine identity.

As we awaken to who we really are, the divine nothing, we enjoy an eternal reality beyond all the things we normally take to be the self. I see at least one immediate reason why this is so liberating. I venture to say that all people feel weighed down by something. Maybe we feel bad about ourselves because we're overweight or because we don't have the talents that our culture prizes to be most valuable. Unfortunately, the burdens of what society judges worthwhile are foisted upon everyone. If we do not measure up, we are condemned to be worthless. I remember feeling great shame when a woman casually remarked that no one should trust a person who is a virgin in their twenties. They had to be weird. Well, that was me!

27. Eckhart, *Meister Eckhart: The Essential Sermons*, 281.

28. Keating, *Open Mind, Open Heart*, 127.

Shame can rear its ugly head in all manner of ways, but it always has to do with our sense of self. Cultural expectations, whether about gender or race or belief, can instill the feeling that I am somehow bad or inferior. To realize the self is the divine nothing is to know these cultural expectations can never define our truest self. It frees us from the awful burden of living up to other people's standards. We can be ourselves, with all our gifts and personality traits, in the most authentic manner possible because we know that our essence is the divine nothing.

SAMWELL TARLY

The second way our identity as the divine nothing liberates us is best told through two connected scenes from the HBO fantasy epic *Game of Thrones*. The scenes revolve around a supporting character named Samwell Tarly. In the first scene, Samwell is travelling with a woman named Gilly and her unnamed infant son. Sam is helping them get to safety. They are both aware of the show's chief danger: snow zombies called "white walkers." As they travel, Sam finds a shack where they can stay for the night. Only, a white walker comes to the shack to get the baby. Sam, not known as a fighter, uses a blade of dragon glass—one of only a few weapons that can kill a white walker—and destroys the monster.

The second scene occurs in the middle of a battle. When Sam gets back to his castle, he tells the men he destroyed a white walker and no one believes him. As Sam is helping a friend defend the castle from invaders, his friend asks about Sam's experience with the white walker. Both are terrified of the advancing army and suspect they will be dead in moments. Sam's friend asks how he could have possibly killed a white walker. Sam replies, "I wasn't Samwell Tarly anymore . . . I was nothing at all. When you're nothing at all, there's no more reason to be afraid." His friend retorts, "But, you're afraid now." Sam says, "Yes, well, I'm not nothing anymore."

He felt nothing when he defended Gilly and her baby from the white walker. His interior was just nothing. His false identity slipped away for a precious few moments, he realized his true existence as the nothing, and he was free. But, once his ego reformed, fear returned.

The themes of death and fear hit viewers in the face in nearly every episode of *Game of Thrones*. Sam found the secret to escaping the paralyzing fear of death: nothingness. When we are nothing, we will not be afraid. We fear the ultimate nothing, death, but when we are the divine nothing, there is nothing to fear! Finley writes that the point of spirituality is for a person to discover that "the nothingness he fears is, in fact, the treasure he longs for."[29] The story of Samwell Tarly from *Games of Thrones* gives flesh to this point. Telling the story of how he killed a white walker, Sam says his inside was nothing. He had no fear because he was nothing within. Even the fear of death wasn't there. He was free of it.

Samwell Tarly says something important. In his state of nothingness, he reports that he was not himself. Who he thought he was fell away and when his ego-identity disappeared, even for a moment, fear disappeared, too. This provides us a key insight: If the indistinct nothingness beyond all gods is who we really are, then the spiritual life is not about adding things, practices, or religious observances. Instead, Eckhart's detachment, understood as subtraction, takes on central importance. He says "God is not found in the soul by adding anything, but by a process of subtraction."[30] We discover ourselves in the same way. In finding our truest selves, we also find God. We subtract all the things from our lives with which we identify until we are reduced to the godless nothingness we have always already been. This is the self that never dies. The divine nothing is God as eternal and transcendent, beyond all things. This is our core reality, too, by God's gracious love. We can rejoice! We have the truly wondrous gift of nothing within us, and knowing this—giving birth to the Word—is pure bliss.

THE PATH OF NOTHINGNESS

The last two meanings of nothing refer, I think, to the way and the practical exercise of nothingness. I want to discuss it in terms of the path of nothingness and the practice of nothingness. The next phrase from Sermon 71, "In all things he saw nothing but God," refers to the path of nothingness. What does it mean to refer to nothingness as a path? Of what does this path consist? It consists of seeing God in all things and subtracting all distinction. Eckhart tells us that nothingness means seeing nothing but God in all things, which implies the removal of the distinction in our minds between God and creatures. It is the path Eckhart wants us to take if we are to know who we really are and, at the same time, know who God really is. Beyond any mere act of the will, we realize our truest self when we subtract the

---

29. Finley, *Merton's Palace of Nowhere*, 111.

30. Fox, *Passion for Creation*, 183.

impulse to be something particular in order to dissolve in the God beyond God.

Eckhart doesn't want us only to let go of our bad habits or our bad attitudes. Detachment means much more than that. Detachment means to let go of distinction. It is detachment from difference, from anything that makes us stand out or appear unique. It is about letting go of our over-identification with our roles, histories, accomplishments, and loved ones.

I grew up with a fair amount of Italian and New York pride in the 80's and 90's on Long Island. Even though now I am more liberal in my thinking, back then I remember rooting for George Bush, Sr., to win the 1988 presidential race. My family was hoping Bush would be president, so I was, too. I also went to Catholic school all my life—even graduate school! So, I never knew many people who weren't Catholic. Naturally, I assumed anyone like me—Italian, New Yorker, Catholic, rooting for Bush, Sr.—was the best. How stupid! Each one of those identities is but a mask.

Nothingness is a profound dis-identification. Our sole spiritual task is to let go of the self, to peel away the layers of the false self until we discover the nothingness beyond God that we are. One is to let the ego self-annihilate by shedding its attachments. It's like peeling away layers of an onion until the whole onion is gone and you're left with nothing. Charlotte Radler says, "a detached human being removes layer after layer of its constructed pseudo-self until it uncovers the true core of itself, that is, the transcendent nothingness which is also God, and only then can it become this same transcendent nothingness."[31] Various layers of identity-attachments hide the true core of our humanity, and thinking that being Italian is the best of all nationalities is a good example.

Eckhart's call to let go, then, is the call to sink down out of the separate self, out of distinction, into the indistinct nothingness of God. As scholar Frank Tobin puts it:

> Hence, when Eckhart says that man must rid himself of *eigenschaft*, he is not only castigating a possessive attitude toward things which enslave man; he is also implying that man must transcend his very nature which is bound by time, space, and other limiting characteristics so that he may become godlike and hence capable of union with God.[32]

---

31. Radler, "Losing the Self," 113.

32. Frank Tobin, "Eckhart's Mystical Use of Language," 160.

So, stop clinging to the self! Stop holding on to the ego-self as a separate and self-contained individual. Whenever we attempt to mark ourselves off as different or try to make ourselves stand out, we strengthen the self that is cut-off from God. The path of nothing is a call to let go of everything that keeps us self-preoccupied. Once we let go of the cut-off and distant self, the cut off and distant God disappears, too.

SOMETHING-NESS

The letting go of distinction translates to letting go of *something-ness*. Our egos and their thinking are the major "somethings" blocking the realization of divine nothingness. Eckhart says, "Whoever wants to be this or that wants to be something, but detachment wants to be nothing at all."[33] We think we are something, that is, something great, big, and important. The word "something" here represents our narcissism, entitlement, feigned superiority, and dismissive cynicism. It is thinking we're better than other people because we're attractive, intelligent, powerful, or rich.

Our thinking is tremendously self-referential. We listen to our egocentric thinking too much, which is the set of voices in our heads creating a separate and false identity. So, the word "something" also represents our thinking, especially the last and most clingy thought. This is the thought of self, the thought of being separate and distinct. The many somethings we experience: voices, self-talk, possessiveness, and distinction. To have any distinction at all is to have *eigenschaft*. To cling to any distinction is to be caught in the slavery of *eigenschaft*. Scholar Denys Turner writes, "Insofar as I am a something for which God is, I am not the nothing which God is."[34] Being distinct in any way means one is still a "something"—an object perceived as outside of God, who is thought to be a separate entity. I even have to detach from self-awareness, from being a distinct center of consciousness and from self-reference.

We need to ask ourselves, when are we something? When do we *think* we are something? When we are something, when we are a being, we stand over against God. But we are never separate from, much less over against, God. So, the journey for Eckhart is a stripping away all differences between us and God. We must become indistinguishable from God and only nothingness is indistinguishable and only God is nothing. We journey back to

33. Eckhart, *Meister Eckhart: The Essential Sermons*, 287.
34. Turner, *The Darkness of God*, 180.

our deepest and truest self to enjoy the infinite beatitude of the indistinct nothingness beyond all gods. Nothingness is a path. For Meister Eckhart, it is equivalent to detachment. But, how do we practice this? How do we shed our false identities, our something-ness?

THE PRACTICE OF NOTHINGNESS

The fourth meaning of "nothing" Meister Eckhart notes is the following: "When he saw God, he viewed all things as nothing." This take on nothing-ness has to do with how one might *concretely* practice nothingness. Eckhart does not leave us in an abstract limbo to try to figure out for ourselves how we might live his mysticism of nothingness. He offers practical advice for how to dis-identify from all the attachments we want to make a part of our selfhood. Basically, the Meister offers us a way of contemplative prayer both as a solitary activity and as a contemplative consciousness we carry with us into daily living.

When I practice contemplative prayer, often my experience is filled with thoughts. Still, there is an underlying nothingness in my experience of prayer. Thoughts buzz through my head, yet there is space between them, a space that opens out to infinity. At times, I get pulled into thinking my thoughts. An extreme example from my own experience is the fantasy of winning the lottery. My imagination goes hog wild over what I would buy, how I would treat all my friends and family to a luxuriant cruise in the Caribbean. But more often, it is the to-do list, feelings carried over from a recent experience, or a thought that triggers a random memory. Then, I see what I am doing, and I let the thinking subside. Immediately, there's just this immense, peaceful, uncluttered, and indistinct nothingness. I don't even know I am in this nothingness until I emerge from it. Sometimes it's only a split second before thoughts return. Thinking takes over again, I return to the nothingness, and it happens all over again. I think the practice is made up of the constant returning to and remaining in the nothingness. It is equivalent to the silence of Centering Prayer and Christian Medita-tion. In my experience, contemplative prayer is abiding in the state of pure nothingness.

Indeed, one of Eckhart's most practical teachings is that that we should "enter a state of pure nothingness."[35] This is a state of mind in which we are detached from images. We are silent and still within. In this state, one is to

---

35. Eckhart, *Meister Eckhart: Selected Writings*, 225.

"become wholly still and detached from all images and from all forms."[36] It is a state in which we have surrendered our faculties of reason, will, and even our very distinction. Beyond thinking, even beyond thoughts about God, the state of pure nothingness is, according to Eckhart, "the right state of mind."[37] He insists that we should stay in this state as much as possible: "be sure of this. Absolute stillness for as long as possible is best of all for you. You cannot exchange this state for any other without harm."[38] It's the best practice and state of mind for us.

The mistake we make regarding our relationship with God is that we think God is some-thing like a thought, a feeling, or an experience. We think God is an object to which we can turn. The challenge of Meister Eckhart's mysticism is that he invites us to turn to nothing, literally no-thing, because God is not a thing and, even more, because God transcends all being. He tells us to "transcend not only the dimension of the imagination but also that of the intellect. Further, since the intellect refers everything to being, it must also transcend being . . . the soul must also transcend God himself, in so far as he is concealed by this name, or by any name."[39] This is, essentially, the practice of Christian Meditation or Centering Prayer. Each one requires applying Jesus' command to deny self and lose life (Mark 8:34–35) to the soul's interior. It requires unhooking ourselves from all thoughts and feelings, especially those to which we are most attached.

In the state of pure nothingness, one pays no attention to any mental phenomena: thinking, feelings, and psychological experience of any kind. The soul dis-identifies from all self-talk. If we start thinking of anything, the response is to pass from something to nothing. As the Meister says in Sermon 71, "whoever sees anything, or if anything comes to your attention, it is not God."[40] In faith, we pay attention to no particular thing—that's God! Keating wisely observes, "Everything that registers on the screen of consciousness will eventually go by, including the thought of self."[41] Our practice consists of waiting out thoughts. Then, without trying to do or be anything at all and subtracting all inner self-talk, God reduces us to the divine nothingness we always already are.

36. Eckhart, *Meister Eckhart: Selected Writings*, 187.

37. Eckhart, *Meister Eckhart: Selected Writings*, 9.

38. Eckhart, *The Complete Mystical Works of Meister Eckhart*, 58.

39. Eckhart, *Meister Eckhart: Selected Writings*, 256.

40. Eckhart, *Meister Eckhart: Teacher and Preacher*, 323.

41. Keating, *Open Mind, Open Heart*, 30.

Eckhart further describes the state of pure nothingness in Sermon 52. In it, he describes who a poor person really is. He says, "a poor [person] wants nothing, knows nothing, and has nothing."[42] Willing, knowing, and having nothing each describe the different ways we enter nothingness. The "having," for Eckhart, denotes being a distinct center of consciousness or self-consciousness. Whether we are willing, knowing, or having, we center on the nothingness here, now, and within. If we find we are trapped in a desire, want nothing. If we get caught in an opinion, know nothing. If we feel too self-conscious, have nothing. Distractions and caring too much about my own wants get tangled into knots of addictive desires. Too much knowledge, opinions, and assumptions get twisted into obsessive knowledge. Self-consciousness enhanced, reinforced, and stroked rots into narcissism. Therefore, whenever these experiences happen, we are advised to abide in the state of pure nothingness.

Eckhart raises a subtle point in Sermon 52. He notes that we aren't aware of God like we're aware of things. It means sometimes—maybe most of the time—we don't sense, feel, or even become aware of God. Eckhart reminds us that it's not in our power to be aware of God and that the highest divine knowing goes beyond this awareness. He tells us to know nothing, and the one who knows nothing "should be so free of all knowing that he does not know or experience or grasp that God lives in him."[43] We are not aware of a divine object; we are not aware of any-*thing* at all. It is only silence and stillness. But, how does one slip into this state?

SINK INTO THE INDISTINCT NOTHINGNESS

In Sermon 83, the Meister preaches, "we should eternally sink down, out of 'something' into 'nothing.'"[44] This is how we enter the state of pure nothingness. This little word, "sink," suggests a delightful effortlessness. It means letting go of self without clinging. We gently choose to let God be God without forcing it. If we let ourselves flow away into the love of God, we are reborn. Sinking implies a letting go of trying and of self-initiated action. We sink when we let go of all our thoughts and feelings and consent to God being God. The ego then dissolves as the divine breaks through our

---

42. Eckhart, *Meister Eckhart: The Essential Sermons*, 199.

43. Eckhart, *Meister Eckhart: The Essential Sermons*, 201.

44. Eckhart, *Meister Eckhart: The Essential Sermons*, 208.

selfishness. It hinges, though, on our unhesitating willingness to drop down gently.

Eckhart teaches us to sink down *out of* everything that is the self, and to sink down *into* God's self-identity and nameless nothingness. We become silent within, let go, and wait for our birth as the divine nothing. It is a sinking down out of ego, out of all distinction, and out of self-consciousness. Eckhart expounds:

> You ought to sink down out of all your your-ness, and flow into his his-ness, and your "yours" and his "his" ought to become one "mine," so completely that you with him perceive forever his un-created is-ness, and his nothingness, for which there is no name.[45]

Sinking into the indistinct nothingness refers to dis-identifying with thinking and simultaneously identifying with the God beyond God. This is a flowing movement away from ego. Birthing the realization of identity with the divine nothing requires it since any action more forceful only strengthens the illusory sense of separation from God. The soul reaches a critical threshold of transformation by not paying attention to the self. But, when we think of self, we are to sink into the indistinct nothingness. Keating teaches that "the basic principle for handling [thoughts] in this prayer is this: Resist no thought, hang on to no thought, react emotionally to no thought. Whenever an image, feeling, reflection, or experience attracts your attention, return to the sacred word."[46] The method of Centering Prayer can be described as sinking into the indistinct nothingness by not resisting, retaining, or reacting to any thoughts but remaining in God through interior silence. This takes place both at the time of prayer and in daily life.

Truly, we are transformed when faced with situations not of our choosing. Realizing that the self is the divine nothing requires trials, disappointments, suffering, and weakness. When the soul experiences these things, it is best for it to sink into the indistinct nothingness. This sinking must occur continuously, which means that in daily life we aren't resisting, retaining, or reacting in whatever experience comes our way. When I do resist, retain, react, I reinforce the ego-self, and thereby separate from God. The soul, then, is to sink into nothingness throughout the day by nonresistance, nonretention, and nonreaction. In other words, as Eckhart says, the

45. Eckhart, *Meister Eckhart: The Essential Sermons*, 207.
46. Keating, *Open Mind, Open Heart*, 127.

soul is to "be void as a desert."[47] One walks around as a clean slate, porous to reality.

To sink down out of ego into the indistinct nothingness is a hard task for the soul. It is like trying to stay put in the desert outside Las Vegas. We're easily seduced into turning our backs on the nothingness of the desert and heading into Las Vegas to indulge ourselves in all its pleasure. The city is a thorough fantasy. We go there to escape our real lives. Las Vegas is a symbol of how we easily we can become distracted from the divine nothingness of the desert, of how we are trained to pay attention only to the surface, to glitz and glamour. Still, Las Vegas can't deliver on the promise of Meister Eckhart's mysticism: the paradise of identity with the godless nothingness.

THE NOTHINGNESS OF THE ORDINARY

All of Meister Eckhart's mystical themes lead one back into daily life, indeed into the heart of daily life. "The state of pure nothingness" is the state of seeing "nothing but God" right where I am, that is, in the middle of the business of the everyday. Every image, metaphor, and spiritual topic Eckhart raises throughout his writings ties into both nothingness and living as the divine nothing in daily life.

Therefore, we can understand nothingness as a synonym for the ground. In the one ground, God and the soul are identical. God's ground is my ground. We let go by becoming nothing. As we let go, the divine nothing breaks through our separate self with its separate God. Then, by sinking into nothing, God is born in the soul. The birth happens when the soul is divested of itself. What is born is the realization of identity with the divine nothing. A life without why follows. Justice and mercy are continually born in the person who has realized the soul is truly the divine nothing.

In Sermon 71, when Eckhart says of St. Paul, "He saw nothing but God," he is talking about realizing the divine nothingness. It is when the divine nothing becomes real for us, the defining reality of our lives. It is being convinced that one's deepest self is the divine nothing. By letting our minds rest from thinking, we receive this startlingly transformative gift. All the major symbols of Meister Eckhart's mysticism tie into this realization. Indeed, the whole thrust of religion is to act as a midwife to the birth. It is a universe-altering transformation from the dualistic mind to the contemplative mind, from oppositional seeing to unity-seeing. It is not that

47. Eckhart, *The Complete Mystical Works of Meister Eckhart*, 52.

we do not see creatures for what they are (i.e., creatures). Rather, we see them first as they are in God, which is divine. Then, abiding in the state of pure nothingness, we await the realization that totally revolutionizes our ordinary lives.

Still, for Meister Eckhart, the practice of nothingness is fully achievable in everyday life. Amidst the mundane work of cleaning dishes, doing the laundry, commuting, collaborating with co-workers, making dinner for one's family, and the rituals of getting ready for work and getting ready for bed, one remains in the state of pure nothingness. One sinks and discovers that divine identity in the normal routines of the ordinary.

The ordinary is what we try to escape either through distracting ourselves with media, experiencing something spectacular, or trying to get what we want. The main culprit I find I use to escape the ordinary is my technology. The point, then, is to start by choosing one everyday activity and doing it in the mindset of seeing nothing but the infinite and eternal God beyond God. As a summary formula, I think a good description of detachment according to Meister Eckhart is *constant and consistent interior nothingness*. How do we abandon all things or surrender? Constant, consistent nothingness within is the answer.

Do not waiver from it; let your interior world be void, desert, and still. Practice this interior nothingness always and everywhere. Allow it, enter it under all circumstances. When you notice you've gotten caught up in an attachment, a passing mental phenomenon, just return with all gentleness to the state of pure nothingness. This is the same as the discipline of Centering Prayer, which uses a sacred word to renew loving intention for God alone.

> When you become aware that you are thinking about or engaged with some thought, return to the sacred word as the expression of your intent. The effectiveness of this prayer does not depend on how distinctly you say the sacred word or how often, but rather on the gentleness with which you introduce it in the beginning and the promptness with which you return to it when you are engaged mentally or emotionally with some thought.[48]

As the sacred word drops, you swim in nothing but silence. You become fully present and intentional in this spiritual state. You realize oneness with God in the ground and live in divine love. Through constant, consistent interior nothingness, you realize your divine identity.

48. Keating, *Open Mind, Open Heart*, 121–22.

For Meister Eckhart, the whole of the spiritual life moves towards realizing the self is the divine nothing by sinking down out of the ego with its false identities and into the indistinct godless nothing. Detachment means cutting off all attachments, and the primary attachment is the self. So, to let go, to detach, is to remove all the layers of self-identity until nothing is left. That nothing is the God beyond God, who is the soul's true nature in the one ground. With infinite bliss, the soul realizes the self is the indistinct godless nothing. This is the soul's infinite liberation, a birth into new life.

REFLECTION QUESTIONS

1. How can you practice sinking into nothingness?

2. Is there anything in this chapter you don't like? Anything to which you feel resistant?

3. Are there times in your life when you instinctively inhabit the state of pure nothingness?

5

The Merchant Mind

GEORGE A. ROMERO LAUNCHED a whole genre of movies when he released his slew of zombie films in the 1970's. Interestingly, these horror films carried a social critique. One such film is *Dawn of the Dead*. The premise of the movie is that a group of people get stuck in a mall while the zombie apocalypse terrorizes the world. The mall is filled with zombies. The group must fend for themselves as they await rescue. To survive, some members of the group venture into the mall to get supplies. The characters Peter and Roger escape a bunch of zombies to wind up in JCPenny. Once there, Roger asks Peter, "How are we gonna get back?" Peter flippantly answers, "Who the hell cares? Let's go shopping first!" The scene displays the raw addictive power of consumerism.

Even more, though, the zombies in *Dawn of the Dead* are mindless and only running on an automatic need to feed. They are vivid symbols of both unconsciousness and the violence erupting from such unconsciousness. We are these zombies who unquestioningly consume, abuse, and throwaway. We do so without awareness. We do so assuming this is how we will be happy. The zombies, though, are not only unconscious but hungry, violent, and dead. They are horrific representations of the base drives of consumer culture. We are all zombies when we give in to the need to consume, to feed. It rests on the smoke and mirrors of advertising that keeps us unconscious. We don't know what we're doing when we consume so much so quickly. We don't realize the costs of rampant consumerism in terms of losing our humanity, destroying the earth, oppressing the poor, and disconnecting from God.

Meister Eckhart has a lot of wisdom to offer our consumer-oriented world. In Sermon 59, he notes how we already have the spirit of wisdom, that is, we're always already one with God. But, we let other things occupy us. He questions what we value. Are we concerned about money, physical well-being, and security instead of God? Our hearts often feel a tug-of-war between the things of the world and God. Television and the internet entice us to idolize the wealthy, famous, and sexy. Hearing about their lives, and perhaps the lives of others closer to us, we compare. We find ourselves coming up short based on the standards set by the culture, the wealthy and famous, or neighbors who just seem to be perfect. So, says Eckhart, we invite in "health, wealth, and pleasure" rather than the spirit of wisdom.[1] This means we let these things occupy our minds and miss God. If we let these things occupy us to an obsessive degree, the spirit of wisdom is prevented from entering us.

Consumer culture encourages such a fanatical preoccupation with the things of the world, which obscures love and reality. If we cannot pull our attention away from the things of the world, we will increasingly grow attached to them. An obsessive pursuit of them will grow. "Health, wealth, and pleasure" could be a slogan for consumerism. It does not necessarily create caring people but often addicts who are out for their own gain. Eckhart offers a solution: nothing but God. Whenever we find ourselves preoccupied, caught up in "health, wealth, and pleasure," we should return to the spiritual state of being centered on nothing but God. Paying attention to God is crucial.

THE MERCHANT MIND OF SERMON ONE

In Sermon One, Meister Eckhart comments on the Gospel story of Jesus driving out merchants from the temple. He likens the human soul to the temple and the merchants to a particular mentality, namely, making God into a commodity:

> Who were the people who were buying and selling in the temple, and who are they still? Now listen to me closely! I shall preach now without exception only about good people . . . all those people are merchants who shun great sins and would like to be good and do

1. Eckhart, *Meister Eckhart: Teacher and Preacher*, 307.

85

good deeds in God's honor, such as fasts, vigils, prayers, and similar good deeds of all kinds. They do these things so that our Lord may give them something, or so that God may do something dear to them. All these people are merchants. This is more or less to be understood since they wish to give one thing in return for another. In this way they wish to bargain with our Lord.[2]

Consumerism is a core phenomenon in our culture. We internalize consumerism every day. In fact, we've incorporated it into our religious lives. The Meister calls it the merchant mind, which seeks to earn something for the self by means of buying and selling. If we are honest with ourselves, this is a normal part of our consciousness. How often are we in merchant mode? We conduct business transactions every single day. The merchant mind is the mind that believes shopping is the answer. It finds fulfillment in consuming objects. Consumer culture trains our minds to discard the recent purchase for the next new thing, cultivating an unhealthy disconnection from products, production, and the producers. This creates a throwaway culture. Oddly, there is no attachment to things as much as an attachment to consuming.

The Meister says merchants use God to get something else, which is what they *actually* want. We can act like these merchants today as well. Sometimes we pray wanting good health more than God's own self, for instance. We treat God like a magic genie who can grant our deepest desires. Eckhart criticizes this view. It means our desire is off, for we want some-*thing*—more money, a new car, control over a person or event, to feel good, recognition, or even inner peace—and not the mystery of God. Eckhart is talking about good people here, not base sinners. Even for many good and religious people, God has become a commodity. They are thinking of their own unmet needs before all else. A consumer is trapped in self-reference. These religious consumers—merchants in Eckhart's vocabulary—are looking for God in their narcissistic needs.

Self-interest functions as the bottom line for the merchant mind. So, this is what it means to be a merchant according to Eckhart: we pray, serve the poor, preach, read the Bible, and go to church only insofar as it benefits us. A merchant is motivated by some self-interest—doing these things to get something out of it. Have you heard of someone making a deal with God? "Lord, I promise to pray the Rosary every night if you send me a million dollars." This sounds silly, but deal-making and seeking our best

2. Fox, *Passion for Creation*, 450–51.

self-interest is at the heart of our society. It's our economic system! In fact, we learn this as soon as we hear about Santa Claus making a list and bringing presents to all the good kids.

At the heart of the merchant mentality is rabid self-interest. Today it manifests as the idolatry of money. It is a mind that forms the very heart of our economic system. In fact, it's a pervasive influence in our lives. What are our normal concerns? Dinner for our family? The company's bottom line? Our retirement funds? Financial security? At what cost do we concern ourselves with these things? We may not realize how our choices in these areas, among others, both affect the poor in all parts of the world and how they arise mainly from self-interest.

THE LITURGY OF THE MALL

We are not born with the merchant mind. We acquire it through practice. James K.A. Smith, a Protestant theologian, says our hearts and minds are shaped by the everyday practice of going to the mall. He says going to the mall is like an act of worship. The "practice" of going to the mall forms our hearts and minds to pay attention to and to value certain things. He says the mall's values create an identity for us and "determine what's most important, what really matters...such practices are jealous: they want their particular vision of what really matters to supersede or trump all other competing practices."[3] The mall, then, does not abide our practice of the Gospel, of which Eckhart's mysticism is a particular interpretation. The practice of the mall makes "us into a certain kind of people without our realizing it."[4] It hides our inherent unity with the divine.

The mall trains us to see all things as objects, indeed, as products to buy to make us feel better. It trains us to be judgmental, to earn approval, and to seek the kind of comfort that numbs us to reality. What truly matters is the thing that will fix our daily problems. We receive a new identity by this training in the merchant mind, and that is the identity of a consumer, a thing that gobbles up the next big, fresh piece of merchandise. The mall, then, is a specific and common way we catch the merchant mind.

This training affects our minds and imaginations through images of incredibly attractive, successful, problem-free people who owe their sexiness and upward mobility to brand-new merchandise. Because these

3. Smith, *Desiring the Kingdom*, location 1557.
4. Smith, *Desiring the Kingdom*, location 1594.

images are near-omnipresent, they become the standard. As a result, our fragile egos feel a constant need to see how they measure up against these ideal images society holds out to us through ads and mall mannequins. As Smith says, the mall's ideal images "slowly seep into our fundamental way of perceiving the world. As a result, we not only judge ourselves against that standard, but we also fall into the habit of evaluating others by the same standard."[5] The merchant mind is a judgmental mind. The merchant mind constantly judges others and compares them to the self: I'm prettier, she's fatter, he's smarter, she's more successful. No one wins this game as everyone becomes an object, a thing to be used and discarded just as quickly as the newest pair of fashionable sneakers or an outgoing iPhone model. Even God is treated as an object for consumption.

Additionally, we can characterize the merchant mind as a mentality of merit, which understands reality in terms of buying and selling. It is precisely a merchant mind because of the thinking that God has to be earned through good deeds or moral behavior. We cannot earn God's love. One cannot buy one's way into heaven. Remember, Eckhart says he is talking about "good people," not supposed public sinners like prostitutes, gamblers, or loan sharks. Good, church-going, and rule-abiding folk are the merchants Eckhart criticizes.

With the merchant mind, we bargain with God and we seek economic security because we want to be comfortable. Comfort is a basic want in a consumer culture. The merchant mind seeks a comfortable life for the self. Our comfortable standard of living, however, numbs us to mysticism and to the radical social transformation it would ignite. Eckhart's detachment has radical implications for society. He would have us detach from our comfortable standard of living, our distracting entertainment, and our fanatical consumption. We prefer a convenient, comfortable life to a truthful and God-centered life. Do we seek God or convenience? The merchant mentality reigns supreme today, and so the detachment Eckhart proposes as its remedy is needed now more than ever.

Thus, the mall is our economic and cultural house of worship. The practice of the mall shapes our desires, training us to pay attention to its values of judgmentalism, earning, and numbness through material comforts. Therefore, the values of Jesus go unacknowledged and unlived. Consumer culture, then, is a culture of idolatry in that it directs our hearts to worship false gods.

5. Smith, *Desiring the Kingdom*, location 1639.

THINGLY THINKING

The merchant mind is characterized by thingly thinking, to use a term coined by Michael Demkovich. He says that Eckhart views such thingly thinking as wholly insufficient to seeking God: "To the soul that seeks God, all creatures must be a pain . . . Thus for the soul in quest of God, all things must be as nothing."[6] When we see creatures as things, we think in a thingly manner. This is how the merchant mind functions. We think in terms of possessions and objects for our use. Thus, shopping at the mall strengthens thingly thinking. It trains our brains to think in a thingly manner, which turns everything, people, animals, and God included, into objects for private consumption. Thingly thinking twins with our culture's default presumption that the material world is all there is. Our culture cannot see beyond the empirical, beyond facts and figures. The empirical realm we see is composed of things for our use and abuse. Thingly thinking is only reinforced.

The merchant mind sees everything as a commodity, as an object for consumption. This is the basis for a whole range of abuses and it inevitably leads to great social injustice. For, this merchant mind can see people and even God as commodities to be bought, sold, and used at will for my benefit. Demkovich contends that "'thingly thinking' snags us, holds us back . . . If we demand that all of our thinking fit into nice neat building blocks, we will be stuck with just those blocks."[7] Consumer society thrives on thingly thinking, which is the kind of knowing exemplified by brand names, logos, and advertisements. This knowing gives us all glitz and surface to lure us into buying a product. The omnipresence of marketing cannot but affect human consciousness. Our knowing gets based on merchandising. We focus too much on things: the next smartphone, a highly anticipated movie, "merch" that comes with a favorite intellectual property like *Game of Thrones* or *Star Wars*, fashion, cosmetics, a dining experience, alcohol, or a new car.

Thingly thinking gives rise to a society that objectifies all reality, turning God's good creation—whether animal, plant, mineral, or person—into a thing for me to consume, abuse, and trash. Our society is characterized by throwaway, by garbage. Ours is a devouring culture. It is a culture of waste and exhaustion. We have a pathological obsession with acquiring more and

---

6. Eckhart, *The Complete Mystical Works of Meister Eckhart*, 418.

7. Demkovich, *Introducing Meister Eckhart*, 103.

more things even if they are not physical objects but more rarefied commodities like a vacation experience, a cruise, or a European tour.

We live in a culture of objects. Consumer culture is nothing more than a rabid race to accumulate more things, even if these things are people or God. A few cultural examples can show how our very thinking is thingy, is attached to what Eckhart calls "something." For, society molds our minds to objectify. Objectification is the mode of thinking.

An example of thingly thinking can help. Pornography may be the most vulgar way our culture turns women's bodies into objects for our consumption. There are more mundane ways, too. The reality television "The Celebrity Plastic Surgeons of Beverly Hills" is a prime example of this distorted glorification. It showcases a group of plastic surgeons as they shape and manipulate the bodies of celebrities and live sumptuous lives of luxury at home. In the second episode, a mother of two teens about to have rhinoplasties says, "You know, they're already beautiful, but they could use, their noses could use some tweaking." Then, they're not really beautiful. They need to fix something to be perceived as beautiful. The teens then describe how they don't like their noses and feel pressure to fix themselves so they can be pretty.

We simply cannot accept ourselves. We get caught up in trying to fix ourselves, and not only through plastic surgery. We try to fix ourselves through therapy, exercise, or eating right. But, we only do these things for ego reasons: to fix ourselves or mold ourselves into a standard set by other egos. This is symbolic of finding our identity only in our appearance, which describes much of our society.

Our obsession with shaping bodies to fit our desires and expectations signals the prominence of thingly thinking. People become objects to use, abuse, and toss like so much garbage. The Gospel vigorously opposes such a materialistic and oppressive view of the human person. Meister Eckhart's way of detachment unto the breakthrough and birth of mystical identity with God is an unabashed liberation from thingly thinking and the objectification it causes. Realizing mystical identity with the divine nothing means one is freed from consumer culture's objectification, as well as its root cause and main product, thingly thinking.

THE MERCHANT MIND GOES TO CHURCH

Unfortunately, the merchant mind does not emerge only at secular times. It comes with us into church. We can all-too-easily approach religion from the merchant mind. When we do, God becomes another object for the ego to consume and control. Meister Eckhart rails against this objectification of God. He preaches:

> Some people want to see God with their own eyes, just as they see a cow; and they want to love God just as they love a cow. You love a cow because of the milk and cheese and because of your own advantage. This is how all these people act who love God because of external riches or because of internal consolations. They do not love God rightly; rather they love their own advantage.[8]

People in Eckhart's time, it seems, loved cows for what the cows gave them. They didn't love their cows, but *the goods* produced from the cows. They loved the benefit of having cows. Just so, we can fall into the trap of loving God for what God does for us. Sometimes a simple desire to go to heaven can be a rather selfish attitude, because I want that instead of God alone.

Eckhart's simile of loving God like one loves a cow echoes the concerns of a modern-day theologian, Richard Gaillardetz. He writes about the commodification of grace. He observes how we in the church of the twenty-first century have turned grace, God's life, into a commodity. We have made God into *eigenschaft*. For Gaillardetz, in parallel to the concerns of Eckhart, the commodification of grace means, first, God competes for our love. "My whole life will be an endless tug of war between the matters that demand my attention in the daily course of human affairs – preparing classes, buying groceries, playing with my children, talking with my wife – and my religious obligations to God."[9] I split life between secular time and sacred time.

Second, this religion of *eigenschaft* means God intervenes in my otherwise wholly secular life. I only experience God in discrete episodes that rupture my life and render the rest of it totally meaningless. Most of life, then, is seen as completely secular and devoid of God. Once again, there is a sacred and secular split. If I love God like I love a cow, to continue Eckhart's simile, then I only connect to God when needed. The rest of my life goes on as usual without any reference to the transcendent mystery.

8. Eckhart, *Meister Eckhart: Teacher and Preacher*, 278.
9. Gaillardetz, *Transforming Our Days*, 30.

Third, the commodification of grace means spirituality is a distinct set of experiences alongside other more secular ones. In other words, spirituality exists in the same space as being an avid bicyclist or a fan of a baseball team. It is just another experience someone can be "into." Then, the concern becomes "getting" this experience of the spiritual. Hence, one uses techniques to achieve spirituality and does so on the terms of the ego. Spirituality and religion become yet more ego-enhancements. God fades into irrelevance and all the power of the divine spirit to transform is sidestepped. Gaillardetz writes, "religious experience is assigned its proper 'place' together with the other commodified experiences of our world. Religion has become a commodity that can be prepackaged so as to fit into our busy lives."[10] I relate to God and spiritual living, in other words, the same way I relate to movies, sports, or shopping on Amazon. Spirituality becomes just one more thing in a totally consumer-oriented life.

These traits of the commodification of grace also name the traits of a merchant mind. Both are rooted in a bad theology. According to Gaillardetz, our bad theology of God as a supreme being has inadvertently colluded with consumerism to produce an aberrant version of Christianity: episodic spirituality and the commodification of grace. Eckhart would agree wholeheartedly. Scholar Michael Sells writes, "It may be that the modern 'God' is in some instances a form of property, allowing an easy purchase on the meaning of religious traditions, a purchase that can be used to stake out positions and mark off boundaries."[11] God is not a piece of property. Authoritarian leaders like Vladimir Putin, fundamentalist Christians, and even neo-conservative Catholic bishops use God to push their own agenda, often one against women and the LGBTQ community, for instance.

Episodic spirituality is a consequence of the merchant mind's tendency to divide life into neat sectors for consumer purposes. We can no longer see daily life as sacred. Instead, we want to excise all the painful moments and boring moments to focus on the attractive and exciting. Daily life quickly becomes a drudgery to get through, to move on to the next new and exciting thing.

Instead of the way of Jesus, we get fast food religion. I use only that religion that makes me feel good. We see this reflected in the need to get something out of a worship service or a Mass, in chasing spiritual highs as a black Friday shopper chases outrageous deals while stampeding over

10. Gaillardetz, *Transforming Our Days*, 32.

11. Sells, *Mystical Languages of Unsaying*, 12.

underpaid employees, or in the effort to earn points with God however sophisticatedly we understand it. There is an oft-quoted line of Eckhart's regarding finding God as much in religious activity as in everyday activity:

> When people think that they are acquiring more of God in inwardness, in devotion, in sweetness and in various approaches than they do by the fireside or in the stable, you are acting just as if you took God and muffled his head up in a cloak and pushed him under a bench. Whoever is seeking God by ways is finding ways and losing God, who in ways is hidden.[12]

Getting so focused on religious activity, we can forget God resides in the everyday as well. This stems from an illusion that the sacred and the secular are divided. We want our own little worlds where we can do what we want when we want, apart from God. But, God infiltrates these little worlds because God is everywhere. The ground from which we spring is the same ground from which everyone and everything emerges. There is no secular, for everything is sacred. Everything comes forth from the one ground. We are deluded in thinking the sacred/secular divide is even close to real.

DETACH FROM THE MERCHANT MIND

Meister Eckhart's concern about the merchant mind is directly related to our contemporary lives. We scarcely go a moment without filtering our experience through this merchant mind. Rather than seeing reality as it is, we see it through the eyes of the merchant mind with its thingly thinking, objectifying impulse, and all-too-easy morphing of spiritual desire into consumer desire. For, we consume not only food, clothes, and other products, but also sports teams, comic book heroes, movies, political opinions, and, sometimes above all, our religious or anti-religious views. Eckhart would have us buy none of the commodities on sale, but, instead, detach from them all and return to our home: indescribable unity with God in the ground.

Thus, the antidote to addictive consumerism is the reduction of ego and its many false identities to the indistinct nothingness. It is Meister Eckhart's constant call to practice detachment. Nothing but God, nothing but nothing, is the answer for Meister Eckhart. There's nothing to it. Unplug the TV. Stop watching the corporate-owned media. Go into real life. Nourish

---

12. Eckhart, *Meister Eckhart: The Essential Sermons*, 183.

relationships. Stop buying so much and opt out of the consumer system. Identify with the divine nothing and the suffering consumer culture often promises to cure may resolve in unexpected ways.

REFLECTION QUESTIONS

1. How does the merchant mentality work in your life?

2. When are you trapped in thingly thinking?

3. Notice what is happening inside you the next time you're in the mall. How can you let that go?

6

Transforming Our Suffering

IT SEEMS FUTILE TO talk about suffering. Words cannot capture the reality of the human experience of suffering, at least not adequately. Even though I have suffered and have known pain, still my personal experience of suffering pales in comparison to the monumental suffering of people who are starving, being oppressed by severe governments, or undergoing the horrors of ethnic cleansing. Suffering of this magnitude is, in some unfathomable sense, a mystery defying explanation even while we may know the precise cause. Yet, suffering is a universal human phenomenon. Everyone, everywhere, at all times, know some form of suffering. Even more, everyone, everywhere, at all times, wants to alleviate their suffering. No one wants to suffer, even minutely. Hence, the religions of the world offer up various methods and meanings to help assuage the pain of humanity. Like Jesus taking pity on the crowds in need of healing, Meister Eckhart offers his owns response to suffering. As one might guess from this book so far, his response comes down to centering on nothing but God.

Pain is unavoidable, and it comes in many different forms. Natural disasters happen all the time. From a car slipping on black ice and slamming into another car to extreme flooding to tornados, Mother Nature can inflict a great deal of suffering on us. There is indescribable and inscrutable pain lacking any meaning and any purpose. It just hurts; it is just torture. We simply cannot explain it. We don't know why it's happening, whether it's serving any purpose, or when it might end. All these different types of pain bleed into one another and can make any experience of hurt all the worse. The lack of meaning or explanation can turn such pain into suffering.

One day a man loses his job. He arrives home grieving and upset. He snaps at his wife and yells at his kids. He starts to drink and only gets worse with each beer drunk. He sinks into a deep depression and contemplates how it all could have gotten so bad. He worries about how his family will eat, how they will live, or how long they will be able to stay in their home. Of course, his wife's cancer comes to mind immediately. What about her medical bills? How will he and the kids get along without her?

This man is suffering. Who among us cannot identify with what he's going through? I have acted worse over smaller things. Who among us hasn't exported their own pain? Who hasn't taken out their internal sufferings on the people around them? We do it all the time. And, we do it because we need an outlet. We feel we need to release our suffering. We don't like to suffer. No sooner do we get a headache than we reach for aspirin. We are conditioned to avoid fear, pain, and suffering. We want to get rid of it. But, how? The response of the man in the story only creates more suffering. How can we negotiate this problem of suffering?

Meister Eckhart knew pain. He also knew how to console someone in pain. The best consolation for the medieval Dominican was to offer the truth, namely, that we are one with God, and if we center on nothing but God we will not suffer. He discussed these ideas in *The Book of Divine Consolation*, which is a long reflection about suffering and how to deal with it. He has recourse to a few scriptures throughout the *Book*, in particular, "Blessed are they that suffer for righteousness' sake" (Matt 5:10), "Blessed are the poor in spirit: (Matt 5:3), and Psalm 34:17 about God being with a good person in his or her sufferings. His Book is part of a venerable tradition in the ancient and medieval world, namely, the tradition of consolation literature.

> In the late ancient and medieval world, consolation literature offered an influential interpretation and art of suffering. This literature includes letters, treatises, and funeral orations . . . They address anxiety and grief in the face of misfortune, illness, and especially death.[1]

Both ancient Roman authors like Cicero and Seneca and saints like Ambrose and Jerome wrote consolation literature, attempting to bring comfort

---

1. Duclow, "My Suffering is God," 571.

amidst pain and sorrow. The Christian philosopher Boethius, who wrote *The Consolation of Philosophy* in 524, appears to be the single greatest influence on Meister Eckhart's *Book of Divine Consolation*.

The Meister, in the tradition of this ancient and medieval consolation literature, offers an art of suffering. Not only does he give deeper meanings to our pain, but he also offers a way to negotiate and even transform our pain. More accurately, Meister Eckhart teaches us a way to let God transform our pain and suffering. He sums up his essential point in part one of the book: "in God there is neither sadness, nor suffering, nor distress, and if you wish to be free of all distress and suffering, then turn to God and fix yourself on him alone. It is certain that all your suffering comes from the fact that you do not turn to God or not to him alone."[2] On this basis, we will explore five points Meister Eckhart makes in *The Book of Divine Consolation*. These points are, 1) suffering is from attachment, 2) God alone is our consolation, 3) the incarnational intuition that God is with us in our suffering, 4) the nondual insight that God *is* our suffering, and, 5) how we can transform our suffering.

One more note before diving in to the Meister's mystical teaching about suffering. His consolation may seem rather glib. It may strike us as, perhaps, naïve or just way too easy. We may read what he has to say and conclude his thoughts are just plain unhelpful. We do need to recall the historical context, though. Medieval Europe was a hothouse of pain and suffering: wars, famines, plagues, and not much even close to the modern era's methods of pain alleviation. So, it is not as if the Meister did not know suffering personally or was closed off from it altogether. Pain and death were much more accepted then than today. Also, it is good to remember that the Meister gives spiritual counsel, but not a panacea that will cure us of every physical ailment. His aim is to offer the greatest consolation even as one experiences pain, a consolation that can transform us right down to our ground.

SUFFERING COMES FROM ATTACHMENT

We turn, now, to one of Meister Eckhart's first points in *The Book of Divine Consolation*. Leaving aside, for the moment, natural disasters and unexplainable suffering, one can observe that much hurt, angst, and sorrow result from wanting something we cannot have or not being able to avoid

2. Eckhart, *Meister Eckhart: Selected Writings*, 57.

something we don't want. Meister Eckhart writes, "all suffering comes from attachment and affection."[3] He means that our sorrow comes from our disordered love for creaturely things. In other words, much of our suffering is self-imposed. Eckhart begins here. An attachment, as we have seen in this book, is an act of possessiveness. It is to choose a creature over God. Eckhart's word for it is *eigenschaft*, which means "possessiveness" or even "self-reference," because the self is the primary attachment. An example or two may help to clarify what Meister Eckhart means when he says all our suffering comes from attachment.

One of my friends was so focused on a girl who dumped him that he felt miserable all the time. He compared every other girl who came along to this one, ideal, perfect woman he had, by now, concocted in his head. It ruined any chance at a real relationship he ever had. I asked him numerous times why he wasn't over her. He could never tell me why. He could only say he tried letting go of her, but it didn't work. Then, she started talking to him over social media. They would talk late into the night, even though she was already in relationship with someone else. Sometimes, my friend would invite her and her boyfriend to meet our group of friends at a bar. I always wondered what he hoped to gain by that. Still, he would be so excited when she showed up. One time he even asked me if I thought there was a chance of the two of them getting back together. I said, firmly, "Not a chance," because she eventually got engaged! Once I saw that he clung to the idea that they might reunite even when she was engaged, I knew for sure that he was attached to his idea of this woman. All his suffering, which included loneliness, heavy drinking, depression, lack of self-esteem, and not getting pleasure from even little things like a good sandwich, was caused by his out-of-whack attachment to the idea of a woman he loved and lost.

Another example of suffering coming from attachment is found in the hit NBC television show, *Seinfeld*, which aired 1990–1998. In the episode titled, "The Comeback," the character George Costanza is in a meeting with executives at Yankee Stadium. As everyone is talking, George is shoveling shrimp into his mouth. One of the executives, named Reilly, looks at George and says, "Hey George, the ocean called and they're running out of shrimp."

George has trouble thinking of a comeback to Reilly's insult. On his drive home, he thinks of one, but it's too late. The meeting is over. George, though, can't let it go. He finds out that Reilly doesn't work for the Yankees anymore, so he tracks him down to Akron, Ohio where he works for a tire

---

3. Eckhart, *Meister Eckhart: Selected Writings*, 61.

company. So, he cooks up a lame-brain scheme to meet with the executives of the tire company, which would include Reilly. He then flies to Akron, sets up the same condition of eating too much shrimp, which leads to Reilly using the same line. Finally, George gets to use his self-described "sweet" comeback. Only Reilly gets back at him again!

George is, generally and comedically, miserable. He's incredibly focused on the things he doesn't have and never seems to get, such as a job, freedom from his parents, and sex with a woman. Hence, he does everything he can to reproduce the scenario in which an insult was used so he can put his hard-thought comeback to use. His need to insult back is an attachment, by which he experiences a great deal of anger in the episode. He keeps coming back to the scene, to Reilly insulting him and how he missed his opportunity to get back at Reilly.

The same dynamic happens when we focus too much on success, money, popularity, what other people think of us, or even just paying our bills. Whenever we focus too much on getting something, like a girlfriend or the opportunity to insult someone who has wronged us, we find that suffering increases in our lives. We get so focused on the thing we can't live without or can't live with that we forget God. Negative emotions inevitably accompany our attachments.

What is worse, if we fail to get what we want or escape what we don't want, we complain, moan, wail, throw tantrums, and generally become even more miserable. Eckhart astutely recognizes this dynamic. Reflecting on a person in this state, he sharply criticizes:

> How can he take comfort and be free from care, if he turns toward the loss and tribulation, impressing it upon himself and himself upon it, so that he looks at it and it looks back at him, and he talks and converses with the loss and the loss converses with him, and they gaze at each other face to face?[4]

Suffering in this way is a clear sign for the Meister that we love creatures more than God. His remedy, of course, is to love God first and foremost. If we truly let God be God and allow nothing else to occupy our hearts, then Eckhart promises our suffering will cease.

---

4. Eckhart, *The Complete Mystical Works of Meister Eckhart*, 528.

CONSOLATION COMES FROM
NOTHING BUT GOD

Two central points of *The Book of Divine Consolation* is that God alone is our consolation, and that God turns every form of pain into joy. This may strike us as a simplistic answer. But, there's more here than we may think. One thing to note is that Eckhart is saying we're too much in our heads when we deal with pain. He wants us to be real, to be in life and not to be philosophizing about it. That's one meaning to the phrase, "turn to God alone." He means turn to reality and turn to Absolute Reality. God cannot be found apart from the concrete experience of the here and now.

The saints were happy not because of anything they did, planned to do, or because of something they got. They were happy because of God. They are the opposite of George Costanza who represents Eckhart's point that all our suffering comes from attachment, from what we think will bring us comfort. Eckhart writes of the joy of a holy person:

> [Whose] entire blessedness consists in unknowing of himself and all things, and knowing only God, willing nothing and knowing no will but God's will, willing to know God, as St. Paul says, "as God knows me" (cf. 1 Cor 13:12). God knows all that he knows, loves and wills all that he wills, in Himself and in His own will. Our Lord says, "That is eternal life, to know God alone" (John 17:3).[5]

If we are centered on nothing but God, like the saints, earth becomes heaven. We live in bliss if we give birth to the divine oneness within us. Discomfort becomes comfort and suffering turns to joy. The cost to this life, though, is the same cost the Meister has been talking about, our love for creatures over God. He continues, "if you would receive divine joy and God, you must pour away creatures."[6] To pour out creatures is to detach from them as ultimate sources of joy. Only God is the ultimate and never-ending source of joy.

God as our consolation is the positive flip side to "all suffering comes from attachment." All consolation comes from God and the greatest consolation is God as God is in God's own divine self. Birthing our intrinsic unity with God is how we claim such infinite happiness, and this happens as we pray contemplatively and practice letting go in daily life. If attachment causes suffering, then detachment relieves suffering. As we have seen, this

---

5. Eckhart, *The Complete Mystical Works of Meister Eckhart*, 531.

6. Eckhart, *The Complete Mystical Works of Meister Eckhart*, 534.

is the whole thrust of Meister Eckhart's mysticism. In many ways, Eckhart's whole mystical teaching is about turning our suffering and sorrow into the joy of God.

GOD SUFFERS WITH ME

What then, do we do about the various sufferings that don't come from attachments? What do we do when a hurricane strikes our city or how do we handle a traumatic event like rape or being physically beaten? How do we transform the pain of the refugee fleeing ethnic cleansing? How do we help ourselves when we feel overly anxious or depressed? To answer this question, we listen to the Meister as he reflects on Psalm 34:17 in *The Book of Divine Consolation*. Much of what Meister Eckhart has to say about Psalm 34:17 comes down to a fundamental truth of the Gospel: "God is with us" (Matt 1:23). This is a line from the infancy narrative of the Gospel of Matthew, that is, the Christmas story. Despite Christmas having become grossly commercialized, Christians celebrate Jesus as God in the flesh. The official name for Christmas is the solemnity of the incarnation, a Latin-based word that means "in the flesh." God entered our flesh in Jesus. And, showing just how one with us God is through the historical man Jesus of Nazareth, God in Jesus suffered the agonies and the death of the cross. One of the most profound truths of the Gospel is that God is truly with us in our suffering, that God knows what it is like to suffer as a limited, flesh and blood creature.

Hence, reflecting on Psalm 34:17, Eckhart emphatically asserts God is with us in our suffering. If our hearts are set on God, then what more do we want? God is our ultimate desire. We were made for the divine reality, and this very reality is present to us in our suffering. All God promises us in the Bible is presence, *the* Presence, which is full of mercy and compassion. Knowing that God, our heart's desire, is with us is a gigantic consolation, just as knowing a loved one is with us as we suffer is a huge help.

God is not only present to us in our suffering but suffers with us. God experiences our suffering, too. We might call this the divine suffering, for God does not stand apart from our hurt or aloof from our pain. Rather, God joins us in our pain and feels it, too. God knows what it's like to endure what we endure. What a comforting reality! This means God understands more than we will ever be aware. God understands our suffering, perhaps even more than we do, and so also knows why we do what we do. Instead of punishing us, though, God experiences our pain with mercy. This very mercy is ours for the taking if we're open to it.

Eckhart then asks, "If I am consoled when another person shares in my suffering, then I will be comforted even more if it is God who suffers with me."[7] Just as my daughter can see her mother ever-so-willing to stay with her all through the night when she is sick and even catch the same cold out of love, then one can see the great consolation in God suffering one's own pain.

Just as my wife is more than ready to suffer a cold for my daughter out of love for her, we can easily see how God is ready to suffer with us out of love for us. Then, Eckhart says I ought to be even more ready to suffer with God due to my love for God. Suffering for nothing but God, out of love for God alone, transforms our suffering, as Eckhart notes in the next reason for consolation drawn from Psalm 34:17.

God suffers my pain before I do when I suffer for the sake of God alone. When this happens, then the suffering passes through God first and becomes "pure sweetness." God goes through it first and takes the suffering into the divine self. Eckhart makes the same point in Sermon Two when he preaches:

> If you suffer for your own sake, however this may be, the suffering hurts you and is hard for you to bear. But if you suffer for God's sake and for his sake alone, the suffering will not hurt you and will not be hard for you, because God is carrying the burden. This is really true! If there were a man who wanted to suffer for the love of God and purely for God alone, if all the suffering came down on him at once that all men have ever suffered and the whole world has as its common lot, that would not hurt him or be hard for him, because it would be God who was carrying the burden.[8]

The catch is not to suffer out of the ego but to suffer for God alone and in God alone.

Still, God suffers with us, but not just alongside us. God experiences what we experience. The divine reality goes through what we go through. If we suffer through God, then our affliction becomes divinized.

> However great an affliction may be, if it comes through God, God is afflicted first. By the truth that God is! There never was a pain that befell a man, no frustration or discouragement, however

7. Eckhart, *Meister Eckhart: Selected Writings*, 87.
8. Eckhart, *Meister Eckhart: The Essential Sermons*, 180.

insignificant, that, transferred to God, did not affect God endlessly more than man . . . if God puts up with it for the sake of some good he foresees for you, and if you are willing to suffer what God suffers, and to take what comes to you through him, then whatever it is, it becomes divine in itself.[9]

God's suffering is part of the Incarnation, of God in the concrete flesh of a human being. Jesus of Nazareth, after all, suffered quite intensely. God has suffered.

For a year I lived and worked at the St. Francis Inn, a soup kitchen run by the Franciscan friars in Philadelphia, Pennsylvania. The Inn is located in a depressed section of Philadelphia called Kensington. There, street people suffer every day from hunger, addiction, shame and the humiliation of selling their own bodies either to make ends meet, to survive another day, or to feed an addiction. Others suffer because of illness. Outrageously expensive medications damn whole families to subsistence level existence through food stamps and relying on the good nuns, friars, and lay volunteers at the St. Francis Inn. God suffered as every one of these people. God knew hunger. God knew what it was like to sell one's body to score some drugs. God knew the pain of being rejected by one's family or being so sick and physically damaged that suicide seemed the only way out. God was not just with them but *was* them suffering. The same is true for us.

MY SUFFERING IS GOD

In his fourth point about suffering, Eckhart makes his boldest claim yet. He says, "The nature of God can be the source of great consolation for us since he is pure oneness."[10] God is one with us in our ground, identical with us even while we are still ourselves. This is the greatest consolation because

everything which the good person suffers for the sake of God, he or she endures in God and God suffers with them in their suffering. If my suffering is in God and God shares in it, how then can suffering be grievous for me, when suffering loses its grievousness and my suffering is in God and is God? Truly, just as God is truth and wherever I find the truth I find my God, who is truth, so too,

9. Eckhart, *Meister Eckhart: A Modern Translation*, 16–17.

10. Eckhart, *Meister Eckhart: Selected Writings*, 89.

> in the same way exactly, when I find pure suffering in God and for
> God's sake, I find God *as* my suffering.[11]

This is indistinct pain, pain piercing the very heart and essence of God. If God is our pain, because God—the God beyond God—is our deepest identity, then whatever we suffer, God suffers. When a child starves, God starves. When an elderly person suffers loneliness, God suffers loneliness. When a high school kid gets bullied, God gets bullied. God absorbs and transform our pain in the divine unity.

There is nonduality even in pain. The God beyond God holds all contraries, all opposites, together in the divine nothingness. Pain and comfort, suffering and joy all reconcile in the mystery of the Godhead. Practically, I think this means we can be happy even as we suffer some sort of pain. The resolution of pain may not be the erasing of pain but the transformation of our identity from ego to the divine nothingness. When we realize our deepest identity is the divine nothing, it seems we are at home with the paradox of happiness amidst pain and joy in the experience of sorrow. This is the beatitude Jesus promises to those "who are persecuted for the sake of righteousness" (Matt 5:10).

Grounded in God, the ground that has no ground, pain does not only affect the little ego-me but also the transcendent God. No experience is off-limits to this God, and even as we suffer we may find God is truly our suffering, too.

HOW TO TRANSFORM PAIN

At this point, the reader could well wonder if I answered the question about how one might transform pain. One could wonder if the Meister has an answer for it beyond getting rid of our attachments and focusing on God alone. He doesn't! Still, the Meister doesn't merely offer us platitudes nor does he console us only by conferring a new meaning on suffering. He wants to change how we experience suffering. So, we come to the fifth point about suffering: Eckhart shows us how to change the way we experience pain so we don't transmit it and, ultimately, so we can let God be God.

Eckhart's reflections on Psalm 34:17 reveal a plan for the transformation of suffering. Suffering is altered when we accept the pain, accept God in the pain, and accept God as the pain. Concretely, this means practicing

---

11. Eckhart, *Meister Eckhart: Selected Writings*, 89.

that sinking into nothingness we discussed in chapter 4. Suffering calls for the deep interior stillness that empties self in the middle of pain and stays rooted in the divine nothingness through pure silence within. Essentially, this is the spiritual state of meditation, or, as Eckhart calls it, "sinking into nothingness." Practicing meditation, or contemplative prayer, changes the way we live through pain. It is how we alter the experience of suffering by centering on nothing but God. It requires putting up no resistance to the pain but accepting it in all its ugliness and hurtfulness. We have to go through it and come out the other side without any negativity. That means we let go of the need to complain about it, rail against, or otherwise refuse to deal with it. We still follow the dictates of reason. If a visit to the doctor is called for, for example, then we go to the doctor. But, we do so without resistance, without holding on to something for comfort, and without emotionally reacting. If we do, we simply fall back into the nothingness. It's that simple, and it's that hard. Still, this isn't an attitude adjustment but a process that takes time to learn with divine grace.

Pain is transformed by sinking into the indistinct nothingness. Now, we are not the ones who transform the pain. God does. But God needs the opportunity, in meditation and as we endure discomfort in daily life, to transform our pain. We give God that opportunity to heal our suffering when we are in the contemplative mindset. Eckhart says as much in *The Book of Divine Consolation* when he comments on one of his favorite scriptures, "Blessed are the poor in spirit" (Matt 5:8). He writes, "They are poor who have nothing."[12] He then relates how astounding nothingness is. "Possessing nothing, being naked, poor and empty, transforms nature. Emptiness draws water uphill and causes many other miracles of which we cannot speak here."[13] Nothingness brings us into the divine nothingness, for "being naked and poor and empty of all creatures draws the soul up to God."[14] If we shed our ego-identity and open to God in this state of naked nothingness, God responds by changing our experience. The divine presence adjusts our perception and identity. Then, suffering is no longer suffering but is now joy, because we realize there is nothing but God.

It's likely not helpful to people experiencing pain to tell them to let go and center on nothing but God. They probably won't hear you or won't want to hear you. This tells us that centering on nothing but the divine

---

12. Eckhart, *Meister Eckhart: Selected Writings*, 69.
13. Eckhart, *Meister Eckhart: Selected Writings*, 69.
14. Eckhart, *Meister Eckhart: Selected Writings*, 70.

nothing begins with prayer, which births a transformed mindset that we can inhabit as we encounter pain. Thus, there is great wisdom in practicing with a small experience of pain first. Sometimes life just hits us with pain out of nowhere. These can be golden opportunities to sink into the indistinct nothingness.

REALISTIC TEACHING

I have bad heartburn. It so bad that sometimes I cannot breathe well. My throat sometime feels so constricted that I get worried I might not be able to take another breath. I have to admit that I find this teaching on suffering challenging, simply because I don't want to suffer like this. I don't want to have bad heartburn, so bad that I need multiple medications to alleviate it. I'd rather have some other suffering, or, most of all, no suffering at all. But isn't this how most of us feel? Someone else's pain looks insignificant compared to our own. And, when all is said and done, we'd rather not have any pain ever. This isn't reality, though. Eckhart's teaching on suffering is hopeful and helpful because it's realistic; he doesn't allow us to avoid our pain nor does he permit us to be overwhelmed by our pain. Rather, he wants to show us how to endure it divinely. He also counsels us to let go of what we want in the middle of suffering to let God have his way.

I think of St. Francis of Assisi at the end of his life. He was painfully blind, so blind that the rays of the sun were like arrows piercing his eyeballs. Yet, at the end of his life, he wrote "The Canticle of Brother Sun," in which he praised God for the gift of Brother Sun, the same sun that likely seared his eyes during the day. Here is a man who suffered rightly, who suffered while being wholly fixed in God so that even his pains were sources of blessing. This is a different life! Meister Eckhart would tell us, right now this very life is yours, too. What needs to happen is detachment from creatures and cleaving to nothing but God.

For, the detached life has no upset. "If you truly have God and only God, nothing will disturb you. Why? Because you are totally focused upon God and only God. Therefore, everything is nothing but God to you."[15] That means that even our suffering is God, and it isn't upsetting because we want God alone. The heart has no upset because it is anchored in God and suffers in God. Rooted in the ground, we can suffer not only with God but as God. When we do, according to Eckhart, suffering becomes light and

---

15. Chilson, *God Awaits You*, 42.

sweet, for God takes the lion's share of the burden. All that remains is for us to practice this teaching and see how our suffering becomes divine.

REFLECTION QUESTIONS

1. Where in your life are you suffering? How are you suffering right now?

2. What comforts you about Meister Eckhart's teaching on suffering?

3. How do you see yourself using the teaching on how to transform your suffering?

7

The Practice of Nothing but God

SOMETIMES I CHASE MY toddler around our house with glee. I play this game with her where I appear wherever she turns around. If she turns a corner, there I am! If she rounds the bend of the kitchen, I am already there waiting. If she heads to our dining room, I am one step ahead of her and ready to scoop her up in a big hug. She giggles merrily and almost non-stop as she scurries all over our house, often running right into my arms. This, I submit, is one way to understand the experience of God that Meister Eckhart communicates. Just as I am everywhere at once from my daughter's perspective, God is everywhere. There *is* nothing but God. Just as she inevitably runs into my arms, we cannot help but meet God in everything we do and experience. The only attitude we need is the one my daughter has. She intuitively trusts me and knows I love her. She gives herself over to me as her daddy. Even more than in the game I play with my daughter, God is inescapably present in all things, indeed, as the deepest identity of all things. *There is nothing but God.*

All of Meister Eckhart's teachings lead to the practice of centering one's heart and mind on nothing but God. As we have seen, Eckhart is captivated by the vast mystery of God. He wants to soak every moment in God and he invites us to want it, too. God is his absolute delight, and his delight is contagious. This refreshes our faith. In our time, so many who say they are centered on God are not. They use God to advance an agenda, a morality, a national cause, or even their religion. Many people are invested in these projects *over* God. They do not seem to be interested in God *as God* but only in making everyone else the same as themselves. They appear to do so to control others, to gain notoriety, or to secure a fantastical and utterly insane sense of safety—usually by excluding everyone not like them!

The God Eckhart focuses on, though, does not appear as the God we have learned about in traditional religious education. The God that he preaches seems wild and incomprehensible, differing significantly from the conventional deity of most religion. Eckhart does not present a God made up of thoughts and ideas, abstract and unrelated to our lives. Nor does he present an ideological God, one that validates political views of the right or left. Rather, Eckhart simply wants us to let God be God. His message is to let go of self and its tendency to manipulate and fashion a deity according to its own image. Then, at the same time, let God be who God is, beyond all words and theologies.

The phrase "nothing but God" means that there is only God. God alone is, and everything else depends on God for existence. Eckhart maintains that all creation would fall into nonexistence if God looked away even for a moment. There is no universe, no earth, and no humanity without God. This does not refer only to the beginning of the universe but to right now. God created all that exists, and everything currently depends on God for its continuing existence. I would not be here if God were not choosing to keep me in existence. Eckhart affirms that God alone is real. We all have a fundamental dependence on God.

Because God alone is real and keeps everything in existence, God is in all and all is in God. More personally, God is incredibly close to us. Eckhart says, "My being depends on the fact that God is 'near' to me and present for me."[1] There is no place, person, or experience lacking God. Eckhart is quite clear. There is nothing outside of God. Everything that exists is inside God. The divine is present not only in every natural thing but also in every situation and experience. Eckhart is clear: "God is equally in all things and in all places and he ready to give himself in the same way and to the same degree in every circumstance. The one who knows God best is the one who recognizes him equally everywhere."[2] God is just as present in the tabernacle as in a bar or a grocery store.

The phrase "nothing but God" also means God is the deepest reality of every creature in existence. The divine is absolutely one with all things. Eckhart uses the term "indistinction" to refer to God as the deepest reality

---

1. Fox, *Passion for Creation*, 137.
2. Fox, *Passion for Creation*, 139.

of all creation. He writes in his *Commentary on the Book of Wisdom*, "God is indistinct from all things."[3] He also writes in the same commentary, "nothing is so one and indistinct as God and every created being."[4] Because God is indistinct from everything, God is my own deepest self. Thus, a corollary to divine indistinction is mystical identity with God: "Between [the human] and God, however, there is not only no distinction, there is no multiplicity either. There is nothing but one."[5] He preaches that our deepest reality is the God beyond God. Still, we are fully ourselves. Put simply, we are the same as and different from God. Eckhart asserts a paradoxical truth: God is God, and I am distinctly me. At the very same time, God and I are one. Even though there is nothing but God, we still exist as distinct individuals. There is only God, and this fulfills our humanity. We take after Jesus Christ who is fully human and fully divine.

So, God alone is real. God is in all things and all things are in God. God is absolutely one with all things to the point of being the ultimate identity of each creature. These three meanings of "nothing but God" unpack part of the Meister's main message: oneness with God. Our already given oneness with God is possible because there is only God, God is in all, and God is the deepest reality of all things. Thus, you and I are one with God, right here and right now. This is all due to divine gift and has nothing to do with our earning it.

Every creature has God within. Every experience and event pulsates with the divine life. Whatever part of our lives we think is farthest from God is not. No matter what that part is, God is there. It seems to Eckhart that we cannot hear this truth enough. God is within us; God is within all. All things are in God. So, the Meister challenges us to remain in God. Knowing there is nothing but God, knowing this in our bones, is how we live Eckhart's this-worldly mysticism. For him, interior mystical states are bound to the ordinary world of pots and pans, soccer practice and school, and the "nine to five" workday. All the elements that make up our daily existence are rooted in God.

3. Eckhart, *Meister Eckhart: Teacher and Preacher*, 166.
4. Eckhart, *Meister Eckhart: Teacher and Preacher*, 169.
5. Eckhart, *Meister Eckhart: Teacher and Preacher*, 301.

NOTHING BUT GOD: THE PRACTICE

What is the practice of nothing but God? How do we do it? Meister Eckhart describes the practice of centering on nothing but God in a few terse ways. He says, "If you truly have God and only God, nothing will disturb you. Why? Because you are totally focused upon God and only God. Therefore, everything is nothing but God to you."[6] He also says, "all things become simply God to you, for in all things you notice only God."[7] The practice is quite simple. We intend God alone. We seek God alone. We "delight in nothing but God." This is done within, as a state of mind. It leads to action. Eckhart instructs us about the one who abides within:

> He ought not to flee or deny or suspect his own inwardness, and so that he can train himself to act in freedom. For we ought to keep our eye on this interior and on what we produce from it, reading, praying, or, if need be, exterior activities. But if an exterior activity is hindering our interior work, we should prefer what is interior. But if both could exist together in one form of working, that would be the best, for man and God to work together.[8]

To be centered on nothing but God is to live from such inwardness. It is "the right state of mind" according to Meister Eckhart. We practice centering on nothing but God by detaching from our over-identification with thinking. This is the meaning of "abiding in the interior state of pure nothingness." This is how to keep God in mind, for God is not a thing. God is not an object of consciousness. Meister Eckhart invites us to center on nothing but God by abiding in the spiritual state of nothingness. This is the state of consciousness in which we are simply present in silence. It is a matter of silent faith in God alone. As soon as we get caught in an attachment or disturbance, Meister Eckhart advises us to sink deep down into the indistinct nature of God.

Keeping God in mind in everything means our interior world must be empty of ego. It must be a place bereft of preoccupations. "Nothing but God" means there is both nothing else occupying us and a simple allowing of interior nothingness, even though our minds function normally. While this transformed mindset still has thoughts, everything that enters consciousness is filtered through a primal awareness of God. As Eckhart says,

6. Chilson, *God Awaits You*, 42.

7. Eckhart, *The Complete Mystical Works of Meister Eckhart*, 59.

8. Eckhart, *Meister Eckhart: The Essential Sermons*, 280.

one "should accustom himself to seeking and wanting nothing for himself in anything, and to finding and accepting God in everything."[9] Whatever is happening, whatever work or chore we are doing, we intend God alone and abide in the state of pure nothingness. In this state, God is born: "there must be a silence and a stillness, and the Father must speak in that, and give birth to His Son."[10] When we do one thing at a time with detachment, we give birth to the divine presence.

This focus on God alone means forgetting self. We don't think about self, get concerned about self, or pay attention to self to let ourselves fall into God. As soon as we notice we are getting interested in self, we renew our intention for God alone. Now, this isn't always thinking about God over self. Remember: God is not one more thing, especially one more thing to think. So, we can have a pure intention for God all through our day no matter what we're doing. We are not thinking of God because our hearts are set on the divine presence in an interior silence. One of the simplest ways to take this practice into daily life is to use the means of a contemplative prayer practice. This means, for instance, taking the sacred word from the method of Centering Prayer to use throughout the day. We can facilitate this centering on nothing but God by repeating our word whenever our minds become preoccupied. We can return to a sacred word, or a biblical verse, as we do chores. Whatever means we use—word, breathing, Bible verse, image—we practice as we are going about the business of everyday life. Nothing but God practice is radical God-centeredness set in the state of pure nothingness that opens one to the birth of realized identity with the divine.

A COMMON-SENSE APPROACH

The practice of nothing but God is a common-sense approach to spirituality. It's common sense because it is simple and accessible. It is not laborious or ritualistic. It can be a quite secular practice because it doesn't take one out of daily life. Still, we need to remember that for Eckhart the contemplative and active dimensions of the spiritual life are always an integrated whole: "Eckhart broke through the traditional distinction between the active life and the contemplative life . . . creating a new model of sanctity—'living out

9. Eckhart, *Meister Eckhart: The Essential Sermons*, 275.
10. Eckhart, *The Complete Mystical Works of Meister Eckhart*, 32–33.

of a well-exercised ground.'"[11] This new model of holiness isn't an escape but a deep embrace of God *in and as our life*. The Meister was not locked away in a monastery or hermitage. He was out in the world. It makes sense that his mysticism would be livable in the world. So, it also makes sense to discover God in our very lives and deep within us.

The practice of nothing but God makes sense because it leads to equanimity. Equanimity is about living in the present moment, accepting *what is* as God's will for me. It is a deep, abiding, and interior peace. Many of us desire such calm, but rarely experience it because we resist the moment. The moment is a manifestation of God's will, and we frequently don't want it. Eckhart notes how many of us either totally resist God's will or wish that God would want what we want. Often, I just disregard what God desires for me and, at other times, I hope that God would want to give me what I want. I may want to watch television so much that I do not pay attention to someone pouring their heart out to me. At other times, to use Eckhart's example, I may be sick and pray that God would want to make me healthy on my terms, which, of course, is now! Both attitudes resist the present moment, which is God's will.

The will of God is the present moment for Eckhart. "If it were not God's will for a single instant, it would not be."[12] God's will is *what is*. A corresponding attitude is one of loving acceptance of *what is*. No matter what the situation, we accept it in God. To do so is to be a just person according to Eckhart. This is a person who can "accept all things alike from God."[13] Whatever the present moment brings us, we practice nothing but God by accepting it.

Additionally, practicing nothing but God also makes sense because it means God does not compete with anything in our lives. We can center on nothing but God while doing our work. The episodic spirituality we examined in chapter 5 divides the world so sharply that we cannot relate to God and the world at the same time. We must exclude one. This is not the case with Meister Eckhart's spirituality. We can love God and the world. God, after all, loves the world, too! The practice of nothing but God never asks us to choose between loving God and our families, for instance. We can love God in loving our families. We can center on God as we eat dinner with them or go on a vacation. All the responsibilities that make up our

11. McGinn, *The Mystical Thought of Meister Eckhart*, 156.

12. Eckhart, *The Complete Mystical Works of Meister Eckhart*, 240.

13. Eckhart, *Meister Eckhart: The Essential Sermons*, 185.

days are opportunities to set our hearts and minds on nothing but God as we are fulfilling these very responsibilities. Meister Eckhart does not ask us to leave the world and its everyday affairs to let go into divine oneness.

TRAINING THE MIND

A program on National Public Radio once asked listeners to call in and relate what it is like being middle class in America. Most called in to the program to say they were one disaster—an illness or a car accident—away from complete financial ruin. Folks are barely making payments, using credit to make payments, or defaulting. People today are living paycheck to paycheck. The callers reported how tense and anxious they felt. They felt that at any moment something could go terribly wrong, even though all had paying jobs. I believe Eckhart's mystical practice of centering on nothing but God can help people in this situation. It is a good opportunity to train ourselves in the practice of nothing but God.

As we get anxious over living paycheck to paycheck, Eckhart counsels us to bring our hearts back into God's presence. When we feel tense about our finances, we can breathe deeply and settle into God by being silent within. This requires practicing repeatedly, because we can be fragile and lose God in the middle of overwhelming emotions. God understands and gives us a billion chances to surrender to the divine joy present right under our noses. Still, as the callers noted, living paycheck to paycheck is tense and anxiety-producing. Well, that is precisely where Eckhart would have us practice centering on nothing but God. For him, not only is God *not* absent from such an apprehensive situation, but also God is waiting to heal us of our suffering right where we are. To center on nothing but God amidst financial worries is to drop the control our disturbing feelings have over us and to know peace. Then, we act from the place of divine peace.

This everyday practice, though, needs to be grounded in a more intense and focused time of prayer. We will never be able to recall the inner desert of God in the middle of an experience if we are not already practicing contemplative silence on a daily basis. Hence, we need to set aside time each day when all we do is sit in God's Presence and soak up the nothingness of the divine. Here, the method of Centering Prayer appears as a way of contemplative prayer suited to our times. Other practices include Christian Meditation as taught by John Main and Laurence Freeman as well as the Jesus Prayer. I believe Eckhart would recommend these practices strongly.

He says, "absolute stillness for as long as possible is best of all for you . . . do not waiver from your emptiness."[14] Beyond the practices, he counsels us to pray for long periods of time. We might reply who has the time? Of course, if we're honest, we probably waste a lot of our time in busyness. Instead of reacting to what we perceive as a burden, we might go against our ego and try praying for a longer period of time. It is, according to Eckhart, "best of all for us."[15]

To practice centering on God and God alone, we train our minds to recognize God in all things. We train the mind to see nothing but God by constantly returning the mind's awareness to God throughout the day. In Sermon 43, Eckhart preaches, "The less we turn our aims or attention to anything other than God, and in so far as we look to nothing outward, so we are transformed in the Son, and so far the Son is born in us and we are born in the Son and become the one Son."[16] Training our minds to see and center on God alone requires a habit of practice. We acquire a habit through repeated acts. Habits create neural grooves in our brains that make it easier and easier to keep the habit. Eckhart knows the need for application, for training, and for cultivating a habit. Of the work required for practicing nothing but God, he writes,

> Truly, this demands hard work and great dedication and a clear perception of our inner life and an alert, true, thoughtful and authentic knowledge of what the mind is turned towards in the midst of people and things. This cannot be learned by taking flight, that is by fleeing from things and physically withdrawing to a place of solitude, but rather we must learn to maintain an inner solitude regardless of where we are or who we are with. We must learn to break through things and to grasp God in them.[17]

The habit cultivated is the habit of seeing and centering on God in all the various things and people we experience over the course of a single day. To center on nothing but God requires that we be aware of what we normally pay attention to in a day. What do I often give my awareness to in a day? What occupies my mind? To whom or to what do I pay a lot of attention? Eckhart tells us to use these realities to which we give our awareness. Right in the middle of them Eckhart would have us maintain an inner desert.

14. Eckhart, *The Complete Mystical Works of Meister Eckhart*, 58–59.

15. Eckhart, *The Complete Mystical Works of Meister Eckhart*, 58.

16. Eckhart, *The Complete Mystical Works of Meister Eckhart*, 240–41.

17. Eckhart, *Meister Eckhart: Selected Writings*, 11.

> Yet it is all one; for what we plant in the soil of contemplation we
> shall reap in the harvest of action and thus the purpose of contem-
> plation is achieved. There is a transition from one to the other but
> it is all a single process with one end in view—that God is.[18]

Meditation and practice in the activities of daily life are an integrated whole. This is the constant, consistent, and interior nothingness we explored in chapter 4. It is the right state of mind that is the state of pure nothingness.

Let us take another scenario from daily life. What do we do with inter-ruptions? What do we do when our hermetically sealed lives burst open and we are confronted with an "other": a homeless person, a beggar, a refu-gee, or even someone who just wants a moment of our time? Eckhart would want us, first, to sink into the indistinct nothingness. Then, do what God wants. Perhaps God would want us to see the person and then talk to them. We might be moved to give them something to eat or drink. The important thing, though, is to practice this inner nothingness, which is to intend and be present to God alone, then act according to the will of God.

VIGILANCE

It's hard to keep up the practice of nothing but God. Life has a way of drown-ing out our priorities and overwhelming us with burdens. Even worse, our culture, as we have seen, can work strongly against deepening an interior life. Thus, we need to be vigilant. Ever the excellent spiritual guide, Eckhart recognizes this issue. In the spirit of the Gospel, the Meister calls us to stay alert for God in all things. Eckhart preaches that we should "be as our Lord said: 'You should be like [people] always watching and waiting for their master' (Luke 12:36). Truly, people who wait stay awake and look around them for whence he for whom they are waiting may be coming; and they are on the lookout for him in whatever may come."[19] Eckhart wants us to stay awake, aware, and intentionally open to God in every experience. This vigilance is constant. We can slip back into old habits quickly, in but a mo-ment. Eckhart says, "it is not enough to surrender self and all that goes with it once. We have to renew the surrender often, for thus we shall be free and

---

18. Eckhart, *Meister Eckhart: A Modern Translation*, 111.

19. Eckhart, *Meister Eckhart: The Essential Sermons*, 254–55.

unfettered in all we do."[20] The point is to return to the practice of nothing but God throughout our day.

It may help to strategize our practice of centering on nothing but God by abiding in the state of pure nothingness. What are some concrete steps we can take to remind ourselves to detach and sink into God alone? We can, for instance, take a moment of silent prayer whenever we stop at a red light. We can use post-it notes to remind us to be attentive to God. A note could say, simply, "Pray." We could put a line from scripture or from one of our favorite saints on the note that will help us remember to let go into God. Every time we do the dishes, we can start with setting our intention, being present, and allowing interior nothingness. We could also hang a crucifix in a spot we would normally see every day. An admirable strategy would be to sink into the indistinct nothingness whenever we see an advertisement.

As we already mentioned in chapter 2, Meister Eckhart names three particular attachments in Sermon 12: corporality, multiplicity, and temporality. Translated into contemporary experience, these refer to preoccupation with the body (corporality), busy-ness (multiplicity), and both regretting the past and worrying about the future (temporality). We can remind ourselves to center on nothing but God amidst experiences of corporality, multiplicity, or temporality. Each experience can be an opportunity to let go. When we get preoccupied with our bodies and our appearance, we can become intentionally present and allow inner nothingness. When we get busy and clogged up with too many things to do, choose to practice detachment. When we start feeling guilty or ashamed of our past, we can let go into God. When we feel anxious about the future and start worrying, we can abide in the state of pure nothingness. Each of us can decide to practice detachment before we experience one of these situations. Hopefully, this will help us to remember to practice when we are in the middle of the experience. Still, we will forget. So, we use that experience—remembering that we wanted to detach in the middle of corporality, multiplicity, and temporality—to practice nothing but God *now*. Every moment is a moment to let go into God.

NOTHING HINDERS, ALL PROFITS, ALL IS JOY

The practice of centering on nothing but God allows God to be born in us. God becomes real for us. Indeed, we awaken to identity with the divine

20. Eckhart, *Meister Eckhart: A Modern Translation*, 33.

nothing. In this transformed state, Eckhart claims, we are not impeded by anything. Instead, by seeing nothing but God we draw profit from everything. God optimizes all our experiences. Eckhart assures us that "what used to be a hindrance now helps you most. Your face is so fully turned toward this birth that, no matter what you see or hear, you can get nothing but this birth from all things."[21] Seeing nothing but God means nothing is lost, sin is forgiven, and anxieties are released.

In knowing and seeking nothing but God, we see nothing but God. As we let go more and more, by God's grace, we begin to see God in all things. We start, of course, by seeing God within as our deepest and truest identity. In seeking nothing but God evermore intentionally we realize *there is nothing but God*. God becomes more and more real for us. Then, all things become portals to divinity. All things reveal God to us. Every creature you run across shouts out the name of God. According to Eckhart, the one who "has only God, and his intention is toward God alone . . . all things become for him nothing but God."[22] Those people, situations, and weaknesses that once held us back now become all God to us. Speaking of this birth, Eckhart notes that "what used to be a hindrance now helps you most."[23] Not only are there no more obstacles, but also what was formerly an obstacle now becomes a benefit. The obstacle reveals God. Eckhart says, "all things become for you nothing but God, for in all things you have your eye only on God. It is like a person who looks at the sun for a long time; afterward, no matter what he or she might look at, the image of the sun appears there."[24] Because of a single-minded concern for God, all things show us their divine reality.

When things no longer hold us back or refer us back to self, they give God to us. Everything shines with the luminous Divine Presence. When we awaken to divine oneness, obstacles disappear, and only God remains. Such a person is fearless and free: "no one can hinder this [person], for [this one] intends and seeks and takes delight in nothing but God."[25] This is the person who has realized oneness with God by letting go of self. Thus, the phrase "nothing but God" points to the last piece of this book's theme: our

21. Eckhart, *The Complete Mystical Works of Meister Eckhart*, 59.

22. Eckhart, *Meister Eckhart: The Essential Sermons*, 251.

23. Eckhart, *The Complete Mystical Works of Meister Eckhart*, 59.

24. Fox, *Passion for Creation*, 103.

25. Eckhart, *Meister Eckhart: The Essential Sermons*, 252.

oneness with God has to become real for us. The journey to divine oneness is a matter of realization.

To remain always in God is to discover that all things are divine. The great awakening is that *there is nothing but God and nothing else matters.* This is not the cultivation of an indifference toward all things. It is not just a neutral acceptance of all reality. Rather, when we realize there is nothing but God, all is joy. It is the joy of nothing but God: our joy is in God alone while God's joy is in us.

This divine joy is ours if only we practice detachment, that is, if we recognize and accept our own nothingness. We do not exist without God. Our deepest reality is God. If we accept our nothingness, it will be revealed as the mystery of God beyond God. Letting go of self we awaken to our God-given identity. If I identify with this or that I am not one with the all. Thus, Eckhart invites us to transcend self by letting go and realize *there is nothing but God.* When we realize there is nothing but God, we are all things, we do not identify with this or that. The "this" and "that" is distinction. It is identifying or getting attached to something, whether a physical object, a person, an idea, a way of living, an attitude, or thinking in general. To realize oneness with God alone necessitates a thoroughgoing detachment from all things, starting with and ultimately ending with the self. We let go of thinking, images, opinions, mental activity of all kinds, and even self-reflection. We then discover who we really are. We awaken to mystical identity. That is the core of Meister Eckhart's mysticism.

REFLECTION QUESTIONS

1. How would you describe practicing nothing but God?

2. What are some key moments you can practice in your daily life?

3. What will your strategy for practicing be?

Conclusion

Meister Eckhart's Everyday Mysticism

OUR WHOLE EXPERIENCE IS saturated with the presence of God, yet we do not see it. To see the divine reality in all things, specifically in our everyday lives, is to experience the transformation Eckhart calls the birth. This results from detachment and the breakthrough into the one ground. In the transformed mindset of the birth, we see things differently. We see from God's perspective. We see the divine depths of all things in all things.

Anthony De Mello provides one version of the following story, but here's my take on it.[1] He came to the Meister in friar's robes. He spoke Christian language. "For years I have been seeking God in Christ. I have sought the divine presence everywhere he is said to be: on mountain tops, the immensity of the desert, the silence of the monastery, and the slums of the poor." "Have you found him?" Meister Eckhart asked. "No. I have not. Have you?" What could Meister Eckhart say? The evening sun was sending shafts of golden light into the room. Sparrows were twittering on a nearby tree. In the distance, one could hear the thrum of the market. Brother cook's evening meal of vegetables stew wafted its aroma into the open. Children played in the town square as church bells rung from a nearby tower. The friary cat, Brother Barnabus, purred and jumped onto the Meister's lap. Smiling inwardly, he wondered how this friar could sit there and say he had not found God. Closing his eyes and dropping into silence, Meister Eckhart replied, "Stop looking and you will see."

There is nothing but God! This, I believe, is the great truth Meister Eckhart wants to shout from the rooftops. Everything we think is unholy, profane, or sinful is never actually distant from God. Our hearts, our minds, and our attention may be somewhere else. But God is always already here,

---

1. De Mello, *Song of the Bird*, 12–13.

now, and all in all. Through his preaching, Meister Eckhart reveals to us the inherent unity of the sacred and the secular. Indeed, they were never separate. We just *thought* they were.

> If you truly have God and only God, nothing will disturb you. Why? Because you are totally focused upon God and only God. Therefore everything is nothing but God to you. You reveal God in every action, in every situation. All your activities point to God . . . If your intention is God and only God then God does what you do and nothing can disturb you, neither society nor surroundings. And no person can disturb you, for you consider nothing, look for nothing, relish nothing other than God.[2]

Everyone can live this every day, no matter what the circumstances of their lives are. In *The Parisian Questions*, Eckhart states, "to exist is God."[3] As scholar Denys Turner says, the Meister is not claiming a name for God. Rather, he is saying that *simply to be is God*. "The formula is not a characterization of God, but a definition of existence."[4] To exist is to be identified with God. To exist is to be God. Therefore, we cannot help but experience God.

Additionally, there's nothing churchy about knowing there's nothing but God. It means we simply live. It is life without compulsion. It is life without complications. It is life without external pressure—even religious pressure. We live for nothing, the nothingness of God. It is so carefree and natural that whatever we experience is a way to connect to God. It can be having dinner with the family, taking out the garbage, talking to a friend, surfing the internet, or watching television. *To be*, purely and simply, in any circumstance is to live contemplatively. It is to connect with the God who is inescapably and unavoidably present. All that is required is that we center our hearts on God alone; then everything we experience becomes wholly divine.

Whether we are washing our hands after using the bathroom, combing our hair, sitting on a train, eating a hot dog, reading a book, or hugging our loved ones, it's nothing but God. All these mundane experiences have God at their core. Meister Eckhart preaches, "All creatures are savored by my outer man as creatures, like wine and bread and meat. But my inner man savors things not as creatures but as God's gift. But my inmost man savors

2. Chilson, *God Awaits You*, 42–43.

3. Turner, *The Darkness of God*, 163.

4. Turner, *The Darkness of God*, 163.

them not as God's gift, but as eternity."[5] Savoring whatever we experience as eternity is to see nothing but God. In this vein, Anthony De Mello relates a popular and well-known story about a fish in the ocean:

> "Excuse me," said an ocean fish. "You are older than I, so can you tell me where to find this thing they call the ocean?" "The ocean," said the older fish, "is the thing you are in now." "Oh this? But this is water. What I'm seeking is the ocean," said the disappointed fish as he swam away to search elsewhere.[6]

We don't see that our everyday lives are saturated with the mystery of God. If only we could see that God is all that matters. Nothing would upset us. When we're in God and when nothing else is occupying our hearts, we won't be disturbed or upset, which, of course, is due to our attachments.

There's nothing but God and there's nothing to it. We *think* there's something to it. We presume there's a catch. But, it's all rather straightforward. We live in the now, inhabiting the state of pure nothingness, and intend God. Without resistance, expectation, assumptions, opinions tightly held, or clinging to concerns of the self, we simply exist in God. Meister Eckhart explains how if one "asked life for a thousand years, '*Why* do you live?' if it could answer it would only say, 'I live because I live.' That is because life lives from its own ground, and gushes forth from its own. Therefore, it lives without *Why*, because it lives for itself."[7] Simply to live is to abide in the state of pure nothingness, which is to be centered on God alone. Being so focused and anchored in the divine ground detaches us from all the things we think we need to be happy. Then, we break through our false identities to know the truth: the self is the divine nothing. We give birth to the Word in our souls. All this is discovered right where we are. It is one's life as it is, but transformed from the inside out.

No monk, nun, or friar would hesitate to call the regular routines of family life holy. Nor would they deny that their own spiritual lives might fly out the window if they had to deal with sick children, cooking dinner on a budget, paying taxes, grumpy in-laws, or the never-ending stream of get-togethers for birthdays and holidays. Still, God is in these very details, the minutiae, of daily existence. Seeing nothing but God there, in our normal lives, is what Meister Eckhart preaches.

---

5. Eckhart, *The Complete Mystical Works of Meister Eckhart*, 293.

6. De Mello, *Song of the Bird*, 12.

7. Eckhart, *The Complete Mystical Works of Meister Eckhart*, 110.

Further, living in, enjoying, and knowing nothing but God has a pointed ethical edge. The Meister shows a great concern for justice in his sermons. The truth that there is nothing but God confirms the dignity of all people, for God is one with each and every single human being on the face of the earth. It confirms that God is justice. Therefore, to practice centering on nothing but God is to practice social justice. God is one with all, and we see this. We then know that we must transcend racism and sexism. We must care for our natural world. It is essential that we opt for the poor, because when we realize oneness with God we act like God, who loves the poor. As Jesus said, we give drink to Christ when we give drink to the least of our sisters and brothers (Mt. 25:35–40). It is Christ serving Christ.

There's nothing stopping us from bringing God's justice into the world except, perhaps, unwillingness. Maybe that's a good place to start? Examine your resistance to living from the divine ground, to practicing, living, and realizing nothing but God. What keeps you from just living? What keeps you from the divine nothingness you always already are? Simply wash the dishes while abiding in the state of pure nothingness, a state in which all attachments are subtracted. Abide in the silence.

This is not something else to do besides everyday activities. It is, in fact, doing less than normal because the state of pure nothingness, the state of being attuned to nothing but God, subtracts attachments, expectations, illusions, assumptions, and really all the mental-emotional material we use to filter reality. To abide in the state of pure nothingness is to abide in reality, pure and unfiltered. We only need to practice abiding in nothing but God, which we do by sinking into the divine nothingness in established prayer times and all throughout the day whenever we find our minds have wandered off or whenever we feel trapped in an emotion, disturbance, or attachment.

We need to let go of the presumption that our everyday activities are incompatible with prayer, that family life and contemplative life are mutually exclusive. Bernard McGinn writes, "all activities, not just pious practices, give equal access to God—what is important is the divine intention behind every action."[8] Meister Eckhart's mysticism is truly an everyday affair. He helps us transcend that episodic spirituality that restricts God's mystery to churchy places and churchy things. At the end of *The Book of Divine Consolation*, Meister Eckhart prays, "May the loving and merciful God, who is Truth itself, allow myself and all . . . to find and realize the

---

8. McGinn, *The Mystical Thought of Meister Eckhart*, 155.

truth which is in us. Amen."⁹ In the end, this is what mysticism is about. All that is needed is to discover the truth within, the God within, who is always already one with us. By letting go, by abiding in nothingness, this divine truth emerges, and we are transformed.

Living as the divine nothingness, who is our deepest self, we know indescribable joy and mind-bending freedom. We know, deep in our bones, that there is *nothing but God* and we no longer have to worry about ourselves. In this way, we tear down the mental barrier in our heads splitting the sacred and profane aspects of our lives. Everything we do can be done in the light of the divine mystery, with a clear awareness of God, which is not awareness of an object but simply awareness. Nothing in our lives is cut off from the divine presence. God's presence then surprises us in its specificity, concreteness, and normalness.

At work, God is present. At the kitchen sink, God is present. Making dinner, God is present. Shopping at the mall, God is present. Playing with your kids, God is present. Walking down the street, God is present. Driving in your car, God is present. Listening to music, God is present. It is all rather straightforward for Meister Eckhart: just be in God and everything else falls into place. Cyprian Smith makes an important point about Eckhart's mysticism:

> Detachment from creatures and images, withdrawal into the Soul's Ground, awareness of my own nothingness before God—none of this ought to be restricted to my hours of prayer and solitude; but it will almost certainly have to start there. It is perfectly true, as Eckhart says, that if a [person] has God truly within . . . , he will find [God] at all times and in all places. But the operative word here is "if." Most of us will find, in practice, that we will be unable to find God amid noise and activity until we have first found [God] in inwardness and stillness.¹⁰

Let us, then, be in God's pesence now. Let us begin anew each moment by being silent within and allowing interior nothingness for the self is the divine nothing.

We can sink into God anywhere, any-when. The question is not one of God's availability or our ability to be present in God. Neither is it a question of God's desire. God longs for us. Rather, it is a question of willingness: Are we willing to let everything be transparent to the divine presence? Are

9. Eckhart, *Meister Eckhart: Selected Writings*, 95.

10. Smith, *The Way of Paradox*, 106.

we willing to remain in God continuously? Prayer need not be limited to special times in special places. The moment of contemplative silence in a practice of meditation can be every moment. We can rest in the mystery during activity. This does not mean thinking about God all day. It is a matter of intention, interior presence, and letting go. Furthermore, we do not have to concern ourselves with the future but only focus on this moment. Once we train our minds to see nothing but God, the birth happens, and then all things become nothing but God for us.

Remain in God while running through your normal morning routine. Set your heart and intention on the Ultimate Reality as you go about your business. Remain in the divine presence now and here. Center on God alone, just God. Take God in all things and you will know freedom, peace, and joy. You will realize oneness with the incomprehensible mystery.

The Meister assures us that all people, experiences, and activities become occasions for awakening to God among us, with us, within us, one with us. God became human not just two thousand years ago in the man Jesus of Nazareth but becomes human now in each one of us when we let the birth of the Word take place within us. Each of us can become a new Christ through a revolutionary mystical awakening that Eckhart calls the birth of the Word in our souls. Thus, he calls every one of us to give flesh to God now and so live our truest identity: the divine nothing who, in our own flesh, is the eternal Son of God. We don't have to leave our daily lives to live contemplatively. Meister Eckhart gives us an everyday mysticism: there is nothing but God, here and now, and that's all that matters.

Bibliography

Chilson, Richard. *God Awaits You: Based on the Classic Spirituality of Meister Eckhart.* Notre Dame, IN: Ave Maria, 1996.

Duclow, Donald. "My Suffering is God: Meister Eckhart's Book of Divine Consolation." Theological Studies 44 (1983) 570–86.

De Mello, Anthony. *Awakenings: Conversations with the Masters.* NY: Image, 2009. Kindle.

———. *The Heart of the Enlightened: A Book of Story Meditations.* NY: Image, 1991.

———. *Song of the Bird.* NY: Image, 1984.

———. *Taking Flight: A Book of Story Meditations.* NY: Image, 1990.

Demkovich, Michael. *Introducing Meister Eckhart.* Liguori, MO: Liguori/Triumph, 2006.

Eckhart, Meister. *The Complete Mystical Works of Meister Eckhart.* Translated by Maurice O'Connell Walshe and Bernard McGinn, NY: Crossroad, 2009.

———. *Meister Eckhart: Essential Sermons, Commentaries, Treatises, and Defense.* Translated by Edmund Colledge and Bernard McGinn. NY: Paulist, 1981.

———. *Meister Eckhart: A Modern Translation.* Translated by Raymond Blakney. NY: Harper Collins, 1957.

———. *Meister Eckhart: Selected Writings.* Translated by Oliver Davies. London: Penguin, 1994.

———. *Meister Eckhart: Teacher and Preacher.* Edited by Bernard McGinn with collaboration of Frank Tobin and Elivira Borgstadt. NY: Paulist, 1986.

———. *The Pocket Meister Eckhart.* Edited by David O'Neal. Boulder, CO: Shambala, 1996.

Finley, James. *Merton's Palace of Nowhere: A Search for God through Awareness of the True Self.* Notre Dame, IN: Ave Maria, 1999.

Flasch, Kurt, *Meister Eckhart: Philosopher of Christianity.* Translated by Anne Schindel and Aaron Vindes. New Haven: Yale University Press, 2015.

Fox, Matthew. *Meditations with Meister Eckhart.* Santa Fe, NM: Bear and Company, 1983.

———. *Passion for Creation: The Earth-Honoring Spirituality of Meister Eckhart.* Rochester, VT: Inner Traditions International, 2000.

Gaillardetz, Richarrd. *Transforming Our Days: Finding God Amid the Noise of Modern Life.* Liguori, MO: Liguori, 2000.

Harrington, Joel. *Dangerous Mystic: Meister Eckhart's Path to the God Within.* NY: Penguin, 2018.

Hart, David Bentley. *The Experience of God: Being, Consciousness, Bliss.* New Haven: Yale University Press, 2013.

Haught, John. *God and the New Atheism: A Critical Response to Dawkins, Harris, and Hitchens.* Louisville, KY: Westminster John Knox, 2008.

Keating, Thomas. *Open Mind, Open Heart: The Contemplative Dimension of the Gospel.* NY: Continuum, 2006.

———. *Fruits and Gifts of the Spirit.* NY: Lantern, 2000.

Keel, Hee-Sung, *Meister Eckhart: An Asian Perspective.* Louvain: Peeters, 2007.

Laird, Martin. *Into the Silent Land: A Guide to the Christian Practice of Contemplation.* NY: Oxford University Press, 2006.

———. *A Sunlit Absence: Silence, Awareness, and Contemplation.* NY: Oxford University Press, 2011.

McGinn, Bernard. *The Mystical Thought of Meister Eckhart.* NY: Crossroad, 2001.

Radcliffe, Timothy. *What is the Point of Being a Christian?* London: Burns and Oates, 2006.

Radler, Charlotte. "Living from the Divine Ground: Meister Eckhart's Praxis of Detachment." Spiritus 6.1 (2006) 25–47.

———. "Losing the Self: Detachment in Meister Eckhart and Its Significance for Buddhist-Christian Dialogue." Buddhist-Christian Studies 26 (2006) 111–17.

Sells, Michael. *Mystical Languages of Unsaying.* Chicago: University of Chicago Press, 1994.

Smith, Cyprian. *The Way of Paradox: Spiritual Life as Taught by Meister Eckhart.* Mahwah, NJ: Paulist, 1987.

Smith, James K.A. *Desiring the Kingdom: Worship, Worldview, and Cultural Formation.* Cultural Liturgies I. Grand Rapids, MI: Baker, 2009. Kindle.

Sobrino, Jon, *Christology at the Crossroads: A Latin American Approach.* Maryknoll, NY: Orbis, 1985.

Tobin, Frank. "Eckhart's Mystical Use of Language: The Contexts of *eigenschaft*," Seminar: A Journal of Germanic Studies 8.3 (1972) 160–68.

Turner, Denys. *The Darkness of God: Negativity in Christian Mysticism.* NY: Cambridge University Press, 1995.

Printed in Great Britain
by Amazon